MW00681159

The Biograph in Battle
Its Story in the South African War Related with Personal Experiences

W. K.–L. Dickson

FACSIMILE REPRINT EDITION

*With a new introduction
by Richard Brown*

**FLICKS
BOOKS**

Madison · Teaneck
Fairleigh Dickinson University Press

British Library Cataloguing–in–Publication Data

Dickson, W. K–. L.
  Biograph in Battle:Its Story in the South African War Related with
  Personal Experiences. – New ed. – (Studies in War & Film,ISSN
  1352–6391;No.2)
  I. Title II. Series
  968.0488

  ISBN 0–948911–35–2

Library of Congress Cataloging–in–Publication Data

Dickson, W. K–. L. (William Kennedy–Laurie), 1860–1935.
  The Biograph in battle : its story in the South African War
  related with personal experiences / W.K.–L. Dickson ; with a new
  introduction by Richard Brown.
        p.   cm.
    ISBN 0–8386–3654–3 (alk. paper)
    1. South African War, 1899–1902—Personal narratives, British.
  2. South African War, 1899–1902—Pictorial works. 3. South African
  War, 1899–1902—Motion pictures and the war. 4. Dickson, W. K–.L.
  (William Kennedy–Laurie), 1860–1935. I. Title.
  DT1916.D53   1995
  968.04'88—dc20   94–39883
                                                              CIP

Originally published by T. Fisher Unwin, London, in 1901. This facsimile
edition, with new introduction, published in 1995 by

Flicks Books
29 Bradford Road
Trowbridge
Wiltshire BA14 9AN England
tel +44 1225 767728 / *fax* +44 1225 760418
(as volume 2 in the series *Studies in War and Film*)

Associated University Presses
440 Forsgate Drive
Cranbury, NJ 08512
U.S.A.

Introduction © Richard Brown 1995

Printed in Great Britain by
Bookcraft Ltd., Midsomer Norton, Avon.

Introduction to the second edition
Richard Brown

William Kennedy–Laurie Dickson (1860–1935) was born in France to English-Scottish parents. His artist father died while Dickson was still young, and with his mother and two sisters William emigrated to the United States in 1879. By 1883 Dickson had joined Thomas Edison and quickly established himself as an electrician and skilled photographer. With Edison's support, Dickson was responsible for designing the world's first fully practical film camera using 35mm celluloid film with a double row of sprocket-holes – exactly the same system that is still in use today. The short films taken with this instrument were shown in the "Kinetoscope", an Edison-patented peephole device which was marketed in the United States from April 1894, and arrived in England later that year. It was the Kinetoscope that provided a practical basis for the successful development of film projectors during 1895 and 1896.

In 1895 Dickson left Edison and, after a short period with the Lambda company, joined three friends to found the American Mutoscope and Biograph company. In order to avoid the risk of infringing Edison patents, Dickson designed a huge, electrically driven camera which used sprocketless film 68mm wide and ran at 40 fps – approximately twice the speed of a 35mm model. Speed-of-frame replacement, combined with a favourable frame-to-screen magnification ratio, resulted in a far superior picture, and the "Biograph" show soon became noted for the very high quality of its presentation.[1]

The organisation had plans for worldwide expansion, and with this in mind founded a British company in 1897. In May that year Dickson came to England to work for British Biograph, and from his base in London travelled widely in Europe, providing films not only for the British company, but also for the other European Biograph subsidiaries which were established in the 1890s. When the Boer War broke out in October 1899, British Biograph were therefore well placed to cover it. In Dickson they had the services of a brilliant technician, and probably the most experienced film cameraman in the world at that time. Furthermore, the company already had commercial ties with South Africa through their formation of a South African Biograph and Mutoscope company in 1899.[2] There were also suggestions – repeated by Dickson both in his book and in a newspaper interview – that Cecil Rhodes had become interested in the potential of film as an aid to increasing immigration from England, and had invited Biograph to send a cameraman to the country even before the war began. Dickson's own view of South Africa, and especially its native people, was romantic, paternalistic and heavily influenced by his reading of the tales of Rider Haggard.[3]

Despite determined efforts to cultivate General Buller on the outward voyage, by the time the ship docked at Cape Town, Dickson had failed to obtain permission from him to follow the army in the field; it was not until nearly a month later and after a personal petition that he was able to get his pass. But Dickson was still not a "licensed" war correspondent, and this was not just a matter of form or simple status. Correspondents who were licensed – by the War Office in London – were allowed not only to accompany the troops, but also to draw rations for themselves, and forage for their horses from army supplies. In a long campaign such as the Boer War, where food was constantly in short supply, this concession was all-important to success. Without such assistance life became very difficult indeed, and the logistic problems that Dickson faced dominate his book to perhaps an even greater extent than accounts of his filming. Both the licensing and the subsequent censorship of correspondents was disorganised at the time the war began, as the Chief Censor, Lord Stanley, admitted in a report to Lord Roberts in July 1900:

> It is difficult to report on any defects in regulations concerning censors and correspondents, or propose alterations to such, as there appear to have been no regulations in existence for either censor or correspondent at the commencement of this campaign ... There appears to have been no attempt to secure uniformity with regard to the granting of licences; some were issued in London by the War Office, others were granted at Capetown or elsewhere in South Africa. Nor does much discrimination appear to have been made in the first instance as to the selection of the papers to be represented, and it will be a question in any future war whether or no the Army is to be followed by photographers and cinematograph agents...[4]

Confusion at the top, together with indifference or even active hostility in the field, meant that Dickson was forced to rely on casual favours and the occasional strictly unofficial help given by a few friendly officers. Few, even amongst the more helpful, grasped the enormous potential of film as a particularly vivid way to record and present incidents from the war, although, interestingly, the War Office began using film for recruiting purposes in 1900.[5] Meanwhile Dickson's troubles continued. As early as 8 December 1899 he notes:

I have only touched lightly upon my many troubles. Nothing could give an idea of how I have been bothered and annoyed, despite the ægis of General Buller's protection[6]

He also relates the particularly virulent opposition that he had to contend with from one unnamed "military officer high in authority", who did everything possible to prevent him from filming. It was a critical situation; clearly his original idea of wandering around and going to wherever the fighting was taking place had to be abandoned as impractical. Finding that, if he stayed with other correspondents, "we should have to conform to certain rather harassing rules and regulations",[7] he attached himself – significantly perhaps – to a Naval brigade rather than an Army division.

Like film cameramen in later wars, Dickson was a brave man who took many risks and was nearly killed on a couple of occasions in his anxiety to remain close to the action. Anticipating that the war would be long range, he had brought Thomas Dallmeyer's new telephoto lenses[8] with him, but unfortunately heat haze and dust prevented their efficient use. In suitable conditions, however, striking and evocative films were taken despite all the difficulties, and the film he shot of the Ambulance Corps crossing the Tugela River after the disastrous battle of Spion Kop is a good example of what could be achieved. Perhaps unsure of the state of his camera after the heavy use to which it had been subjected, Dickson filmed three sequences of this subject from the same camera position; quite remarkably, all three versions have survived.[9] Although the Biograph camera could produce superb results, its great size and weight proved to be an almost insuperable burden in the rough conditions of a battlefield, where speed and mobility were as essential to a film cameraman as they were to a soldier. Describing a skirmish after Spion Kop, Dickson wrote of a typical situation:

> Getting back to a safer position, we watched the valiant attack of our men as they gradually pushed on. Had we had a light camera these movements could have been secured, and many others of an invaluable nature, but the enormous bulk of our apparatus which had to be dragged about in a Cape cart with two horses, prevented our getting to the spot. The difficulties were aggravated by the absence of roads, while the huge gullies we had to cross and the enormous boulders we had to get over made the enterprise almost impracticable. We really risked our lives to secure the views...[10]

Dickson never refers to other film cameramen in his book, but he was far from being on his own in South Africa. His most energetic rival was

The Warwick Trading Company, based in Warwick Court, London, and managed by Charles Urban. Warwick used the services of several cameramen; some resident in South Africa, and some sent out from England. Their advantage in the field of battle lay in the relative portability of their equipment, which was hand-operated and used standard 35mm film. Not surprisingly, Urban was quick to emphasise this to his customers:

> The Bioscope cameras used do not weigh three-quarters of a ton, and can be as easily carried as an ordinary ¼ plate camera. As means of Transportation are (sic) one of the difficult problems in South Africa, it can be readily understood the advantages our photographer has over the other encumbered with heavy and bulky instruments.[11]

The footage that Dickson managed to take was more varied than might be thought, and most of it could correctly be described as "actuality". Many films showed the troops in action around the camp (although not actually fighting the Boers – the failure of the telephoto lens had erased that hope). Sequences involving troop movements were often "staged" – an inevitable precaution if a decent picture was to be obtained – and when times were quiet, miscellaneous activities were filmed, such as a tug-of-war contest and even a fight between a tarantula and a scorpion. Only once, in the curious case of the raising of the British flag at Pretoria, was there an apparently deliberate case of "faking". Dickson had placed great symbolic importance on this ceremony – it was, he said, "the principal aim of our enterprise". However, despite making strenuous efforts to arrive in Pretoria ahead of Lord Roberts, he had been frustrated by slow trains, so that by the time he arrived everything was over. Ingenuity was clearly called for in this situation – running up another flag and carefully filming it in close-up to disguise the fact that the square in front of the building was now empty, he rather disingenuously suggested in his diary that the scene was too large to include both the flag and the crowds – a manipulation of the truth neatly controverted by another photograph included in his own book! In any event, the deception was soon revealed, and publicised in South Africa, when those who had been present at the actual ceremony pointed out that the flag used by Lord Roberts was several times smaller, and far less impressive, than the one chosen by Dickson![12]

At the beginning of the campaign at least, films, still photographs and portions of the diary were sent back to England on a weekly basis;[13] considering the difficulties involved, the times achieved were very creditable. *The Landing of General Buller at Cape Town*, for example, filmed on 31 October 1899, was being shown at the Palace Theatre in London by 21 November; *Royal Engineers Bridging the Tugela River*, shot on 29 November, could be seen two months later. Intensely interested in any news from the front, audiences were hardly likely to be critical of delay, and it was reported that business at the Palace increased at a time when most other music halls found their results were showing a decline. Tales of Dickson's adventures soon began to circulate among film people in London, and Charles Urban, no doubt irritated by all the free publicity a rival cameraman was getting and by Dickson's rather frequent habit of "name-dropping", remarked sarcastically that:

> Our operators and cameras are not bullet-proof, nor have we been able to induce General Buller to conduct the South African campaign to suit our purposes. We are "sawing wood and saying nothing" but we produce results, which is better than mere Press puff to satisfy shareholders.[14]

It is not widely known that extracts from Dickson's diary were first published in a well illustrated 32-page souvenir brochure – *The War by Biograph*, which was given to patrons of the Palace on 19 March 1900 to commemorate the third anniversary of the Biograph performances at the theatre.[15]   Comparison with the corresponding sections later published in *The Biograph in Battle* indicates that a considerable amount of rewriting was done and some textual changes were made. This evidence suggests that the published book is not a literal transcription of the manuscript. In other respects, however, there seems no reason to doubt its genuineness, its great value being that it was written at the time, rather than in a mood of retrospection long after the event. Of more significance perhaps is a note at the back of the brochure which states that "A further edition of *The Biograph and the War* (sic) will in due course be published". Thus it seems quite certain that at the time the diary was being compiled, Dickson knew that it was to be published. How far did that knowledge affect the way he wished to present himself, his selection of incidents, or even questions of self-censorship? How much of what Dickson originally wrote is printed in *The Biograph in Battle*? These are questions which can only be answered if the original manuscript becomes available for study.

Despite the very considerable costs involved and the hardships run by cameramen, there can be no doubt that Biograph and Warwick's decision to film in South Africa brought them very satisfactory results in terms of product, profit and prestige. W T Smedley, British Biograph's chairman, reported to shareholders at the 1900 AGM that the sale of Dickson's films to sister companies within the international group had brought in "a very handsome profit indeed" (in fact, over £2000, a considerable amount for that time). Warwick's net monthly sales figures were up by 52% for the first six months of 1900, compared with the corresponding period for the previous year – a particularly good illustration of the beneficial effects the Boer War had on the growth of film exhibition in England. As late as June 1902 the Palace was still showing some of Dickson's war films to mark the end of the conflict.[16]

It is primarily as a record of courage, enthusiasm and human endeavour that Dickson's *The Biograph in Battle* deserves to be remembered. It tells of one man's absolute determination to bring back against great odds and considerable danger, a filmed record of a war, at a time when film itself was still in its infancy and few understood its potential. Dickson, his world and all its once-important concerns are now long gone. However, some of his films have survived, and it is pleasing, as we move towards the centenary of both commercial film and the Boer War, that his truly unique book – the first-ever published by a film cameraman and now a rare collector's item – has once again become generally available.

Notes

[1]   See Hendricks and Musser for detailed accounts of Dickson's early work on cinematography in the United States.

[2]   Registered in London on 24 February 1899. Commercial papers are in the Public Record Office (PRO). BT 31/8370/60838.

[3]   For Rhodes, see *The Biograph in Battle*: 7 and 193-197; and Gutsche: 43n7. For Rider Haggard references, see *The Biograph in Battle*: 34, 41 and 46.

[4]   PRO. WO 108/262 – *Report on Press Censorship*, 7 July 1900. See also PRO. WO 33/198, for examples of muddle and low morale in the Durban censors' office.

[5]   Rachael Low and Roger Manvell, *The History of the British Film, 1896-1906* (London: George Allen & Unwin, 1948): 55-56. The film made by R W Paul was entitled *Army Life, or How Soldiers Are Made*

and was shown commercially at the Alhambra music hall in Leicester Square, London.

6   *The Biograph in Battle*: 65.

7   *The Biograph in Battle*: 66.

8   Advertised and illustrated in the book on page 299. Thomas R Dallmeyer wrote the first book on the subject – *Telephotography* (London: William Heinemann, 1899). Contemporary development and practice is covered by Ernest Marriage in *Elementary Telephotography* (London: Iliffe & Sons, 1901). This book illustrates several of Dallmeyer's lenses, but does not discuss their specific application to cinematography.

9   National Film and Television Archive, Schultze Collection, cans 12, 40B and 45C.

10   *The Biograph in Battle*: 145-146.

11   *Era*, 9 December 1899: 28. For Warwick, see Bottomore; and Barnes: 164-169.

12   *The Biograph in Battle*: 237, 241 and 259. See also Gutsche: 44n8. A detailed analysis of the subjects chosen by Dickson for filming gives considerable insight into his personality.

13   *The Biograph in Battle*: 98 (entry for 27 December 1899).

14   *Era*, 10 February 1900: 27, column 3. Advertisement, Warwick Trading Company, headed "New War Films".

15   This is one of the great rarities of early cinema. Only four copies are known to have survived, one of which is in the library of the British Film Institute.

16   Palace Theatre Archive. Programme for 24 June 1902. The Boers officially surrendered at Pretoria on 31 May 1902.

17   *The Biograph in Battle*, issued in January 1901, was available in a handsome binding of either red or green cloth lettered in gold and black on the spine, and white and black on the front cover, which carried three photographs in a recessed panel. Popular interest in the

Boer War was beginning to fade towards the end of 1901, and it is this, together with the book's relatively high price of 6/- (30p) that is probably responsible for its present rarity.

Further reading

Barnes, John. *Filming the Boer War* (London: Bishopsgate Press, 1992).

Bottomore, Stephen. "Joseph Rosenthal: The most glorious profession", *Sight and Sound* 52: 4 (autumn 1983): 260-265.

De Lange, J H. *The Anglo-Boer War. 1899-1902* (Pretoria: State Archives Service, 1991).

Gutsche, Thelma. *The History and Social Significance of Motion Pictures in South Africa, 1895-1940* (Cape Town: Howard Timmins, 1972).

Hendricks, Gordon. *Origins of the American Film* (New York: Arno Press and The New York Times, 1972).

Musser, Charles. *The Emergence of Cinema – The American Screen to 1907* (New York: Charles Scribner's Sons, 1990).

Pakenham, Thomas. *The Boer War* (London: George Weidenfeld & Nicholson, 1979).

Strebel, Elizabeth Grottle. "Primitive Propaganda: The Boer War Films", *Sight and Sound* 46: 1 (winter 1976/77): 45-47. Reprinted in De Lange op. cit., and under the title of "Imperialist Iconography of Anglo-Boer War Film Footage", in John L Fell (ed), *Film Before Griffith* (Berkeley: University of California Press, 1983): 264-271.

THE BIOGRAPH IN BATTLE

The Biograph in Battle

Its Story in the South African War
Related with Personal Experiences
By W. K.-L. Dickson, Author of "The
History of the Kinetograph" and joint author
with Antonia Dickson of "The Life and
Inventions of Edison"   ❦   ❦   ❦   ❦

ILLUSTRATED FROM PHOTOGRAPHS
AND SKETCHES BY THE AUTHOR

LONDON: T. FISHER UNWIN
PATERNOSTER SQUARE 1901

DEDICATION

*

PREFATORY NOTE

THOUGH the literature of the South
African War has grown so vast that it
would of itself form a large library, and
though it might be thought that every
imaginable point had been taken, every
position occupied, every theory discussed,
the author of "The Biograph in Battle"
may fairly claim to have broken entirely
virgin soil. We are all familiar with the
Biograph, and we have all read largely
about the war, but the story of the combination of the two is a thing absolutely
new in the annals of war or science. Mr.
Dickson has succeeded in biographically re-
producing actual battle scenes. He had the
good fortune to obtain unique privileges and
permits from the military authorities, so that
he saw and heard things which probably

came within the ken of no other civilian,
and by the use of the telephoto, together
with great personal hardship, risk, and daring,
he was able to get photographs of things
which never before came into the eye of
the camera. He was with Sir Redvers
Buller's army through its arduous march
to Ladysmith, and was an eye-witness of
Colenso, Spion Kop, etc., and of the entry
into Ladysmith. While on the march and
in camp he was enabled to be continually at
the part where "things were happening"; he
has been in the direct firing line frequently by
design and on occasion accidentally and almost
disastrously, and his travelling experiences
under storm and stress of circumstances throw
an instructive, though marvellously cheerful,
light on the joys of camping out on the veldt.

The author tells his own tale and not
somebody else's; we are not deluged with
the criticisms, extenuations, and suggestions
which have been so profusely and contra-
dictorily crammed down the throat of the
public. It is not his aim to whitewash
generals or to condemn tactics.

After the relief of Ladysmith he joined
Lord Roberts' field force on the march to

Pretoria, and was enabled to take some most interesting photographs ; for instance, Lord Roberts consented to be biographed with all his Staff, actually having his table taken out into the sun for the convenience of Mr. Dickson.

But the greatest achievement, that for which the expedition was mainly undertaken, and which will preserve before the nation's eyes the occurrence of two great events in England's history, was the recording by Biograph of the Orange River Colony annexation ceremony at Bloemfontein and the hoisting of the British flag at Pretoria.

THE QUEEN REVIEWING TROOPS IN WINDSOR PARK.

LIST OF ILLUSTRATIONS

———•◦•———

W. K.-L. Dickson.   Native.   Jno. Seward.   Wm. Cox.

OUR CAMP.

THE BIOGRAPH IN BATTLE

October 14, 1899.—We sailed from Southampton, England, for South Africa, on the *Dunottar Castle* (Sir Donald Currie's S.S. Packet Line) in company with Sir Redvers Buller and Staff.

Madeira, October 18, 1899.—We arrived at 4 a.m. We rose at 6, and at 6.45 the General and his Staff were on deck, as were nearly all the passengers. We were awakened by the boatmen trying to sell their basket chairs; a most interesting and lively scene which I could easily see through my porthole.

On deck many were preparing to go on shore; the General, however, did not venture, and contented himself with watching the Madeira boys diving for pennies and upsetting each other's boats. Coaling was the order of the day. Huge bag-loads of dusty, crumbly coal creating clouds of dust, and causing us all, and every part of the ship, to suffer. We decided to get rid of the dust for a while, and went on shore in a row-boat. How delighted we were to get on *terra firma* once more, after five days of wild tossing!

Madeira is quaint and odd in the extreme, and the oxen pervade all the streets, attached to queer-looking sleds. The streets are paved with small round stones in ridges to avoid over-friction with the sled runners.

You go to the top of the mountain or hill by means of these ox-carts or sleds—that is, if you are not in a hurry ; or you may take a cogged rail steam-car *à la Rigi* plan and wend your way up through endless villas and small bamboo farms, rising always above the town, which appears to be slowly sinking away at your feet. Beyond this is the calm blue sea, dotted close to the shore with various crafts, our own good boat seeming no larger at this extreme distance than a good-sized canoe.

We tried to get breakfast at the mountain top, where a very picturesque and beautiful hotel is situated ; but we found we had to satisfy ourselves with the perfume of thousands of tropical flowers and the sound of falling water from numerous fountains. The very birds seemed crazed with delight, and were piping their little heads off from sheer joy to be in such an atmosphere. Never in my whole life have I felt such air ; it is surely beyond compare. But for the breakfast we waited in vain, and knowing how much we had to do before the departure of the boat, told the manager he would have to improve his service if he wished any custom, and departed fasting. We climbed a little further, accompanied by swarms of natives— guides I believe they wished to be called—whose one object was to see how much they could get out of you within a given time. The Church of Our Lady of the Mount was our goal, and after enjoying the quaint old structure and its relics we lingered on the broad steps to drink in a scene of wonderful beauty. Peeping through a dark-green foreground of tall pine trees, Madeira appeared nestling at the foot of the great craggy mountain and kissed by the rich blue Atlantic.

Soon we were recalled to the necessity of speed, which we shortly after realised to a rather startling degree. A two-man sled awaited us. We crowded into the one seat and were pushed off down an undulatory road, paved with small round stones. The speed was appalling at times, and often we quite expected to find ourselves in some one's kitchen instead of sticking to the road. The two men behind would guide the conveyance with their bodies while standing on the back runners, and when not going at full speed would leap behind and check and guide us by ropes. Halfway down we were politely invited to taste a glass of Madeira wine and incidentally to treat the guides to the tune of five shillings for four glasses. Our shipmates were subjected to the same experience, as we discovered by comparing notes that night. I would simply add that they received only what we considered them entitled to, not what they demanded.

Returning to the wharf, we got into our boat along with some of General Buller's Staff, but as we were about to shove off, a native, without any apparent authority, stopped the boat and demanded that the payment should be made to him and not to the boatmen. As he was very insolent the officer nearest to him shoved him off into the water, when the fun commenced. A howling, screaming pack of boatmen rushed down the stone steps and tried to get at us. The officer only laughed. As soon as the individual reappeared above the tide, making desperate efforts to get at his tormentor, there ensued a lively scene, a mad struggle for supremacy easily won by our friend. By this time the owner came, and at the boatmen's say-so he was paid. It would make a very funny picture to sketch the man being caught by the throat as he was about to step into the boat, and being thrown overboard, while underneath the sketch should be written the remark made by his victor : " Go and get a wash, you filthy beast." I might add that our friend was Major-General Pole-Carew.

We soon found ourselves on board preparing for the Biograph picture of " Madeira boys diving for pennies, and boats crowding in to get their share." The captain and officers gave us every assistance. Collecting our various snap-shot plates and films, we prepared the packet for shipment to London, facilitated by the courtesy of the doctor, who lent us his surgery for a dark room. It was then noon, and the vessel was to leave at 12.30. Not wishing to trust the packet to any of the natives, we took a boat to shore and chanced it, seeing that the coaling was still going on. Halfway to the shore we were picked up by a tug and towed in a most alarming manner through the boiling and seething water as we dashed along. We cast off from the tug and rowed to shore, beached the boat among the breakers and ran. Instructions were given to rush the packet through to London. As I am now scribbling again on board, I need not add that we " just caught the boat " and had an hour to spare. Humiliating !

As soon as we had lunch we quietly left the beautiful Madeira Isles.

Then ensued a busy scene, swabbing the decks to remove the ubiquitous coal-dust. We were deluged with water, and had to dodge here and there to avoid the hose with its drenching shower.

I made an interesting sketch of General Buller scrambling up on to the skylight to avoid the deluge, where most of us perched, to be shortly afterwards ousted by the sailors who wished to wash down the skylights. When the sailor requested the General to get down he laughingly remarked, " Now then, you wouldn't wash me off, would you?" and nimbly jumped down. Catching his eye, I could not help laughing outright as his kindly and intelligent face depicted the liveliest humour.

Soon everything assumed its usual aspect, and the afternoon passed serenely on into a balmy night, brilliantly lighted by a full moon which showed how fast we were approaching the equator, as even now the moon appeared to shine directly over us, soon to pass to the opposite side of the sky to that we of the northern clime are accustomed to. The same thing very soon we must say of the sun. When further south of the equator it will be curious to see the sun bearing north instead of south.

The order of the evening was a good chat with our genial Captain, officers, and General Buller's Staff, and the other passengers, among whom are included several war correspondents ; at the same time we enjoyed the popular airs of the day played by the ship's band, a band composed of the stewards. The first night we were regaled with a painful lack of *ensemble*, but having discovered that they had never before played together we rather enjoyed their unpretentious style ; so little does it take to entertain one on board a boat.   These performances took place every other evening.   Chess-players, moongazers, and the ubiquitous pedestrian, all have a part to play in a long, tedious voyage.

This morning, Friday, the 20th of October, the General and his Staff took possession of the lower deck, as the heat drove them from the ladies' boudoir which was given over to the General in order to hold their councils of war therein.   So now we discreetly pass by and leave them to plan destruction to our enemies and speedy peace for all.

Saturday, October 21st.—Cape Verde to our left is a most welcome sight this morning as we first view the land from our port-hole, and we hasten on deck, knowing that it will be the last bit of land we shall see for eight or nine days.   Our port-holes for the last few days have been open day and night, with wind-scoops pushed out to catch the air.   I have the top-bunk next the port-hole and have to manipulate to prevent our bunks being washed away by a sudden wave, which having once occurred on our second day out was a lesson indeed.   The port-hole had not been entirely closed, and at 2 a.m. the sea got suddenly much rougher and we found ourselves deluged with water.   My companion, one of General Buller's Staff, occupying the under bunk got the surplus of what I didn't require, and gasped as the cold water landed on him.   We endured the night, and rose none the worse for this long-drawn-out salt-water bath.   Since then, as I have stated, the sea has been perfectly calm.

By dint of sticking up notices everywhere and

getting together a few friends for a Sports Committee, I shall soon be rewarded by having the athletic sports and games. These sports are customary, but it was evidently not proposed to have them on this trip.

Another beautiful day, rather more windy though. The sailors are busy putting up the tennis and cricket nets, and between times hauling out from among the chaos of boxes in the hold those packages marked "Wanted on the voyage."

As the days pass on some of the social chill wears off, and we are getting to know each other a little better. Major Rhodes could give me but very little encouragement last night regarding the near possibility of my reaching his brother; as he fears that it will take months to rescue him from the Boers. He seemed much interested in my letter to Cecil Rhodes and in what I told him regarding my plans, also as to what had been arranged in the matter of opening up South Africa with the Biograph, an undertaking which had been delayed until now for the double purpose of getting war pictures as well.

We are passing through a very large school of porpoise, whose antics we record biographically *en passant*. Their little ways are so well known to the traveller that any further peroration on the subject would be superfluous.

The bugle echoes through the ship, announcing lunch, and immediately the General, a true soldier, is on time and takes his place at table. Never have I seen him late for any meal. One of the officers whom I questioned as to the meaning of the meal-time bugle calls, stated that they were associated with the following touching lines:

First bugle—

> " Officers' wives have pudding and pies,
> Surgeons' wives have skilly,
> Privates' wives have two black eyes—
> It nearly drives them silly."

Second bugle—

" Come to the cook-house door, come to the cook-house door."

It is hard to discover the history of these odd lines and when first they came into use. I quote them here for what they are worth.

Sunday, October 22nd.—Peace reigns supreme; the ocean is as flat as a pancake. What a contrast to last Sunday! The highly interesting and much abused sufferers have no excuse to stay in their bunks and so are seen on deck, being tenderly cared for by their respective gallants, who tuck them into their steamer chairs and supply them with ices and lemon squashes.

At 10.15 we have ship's muster on the lower decks, when all the available crew and officers are present for inspection by the Captain as he passes down the line of men, who salute in turn. In ten minutes the formality is over, and a tinkling bell reminds us that divine service is about to be held in the saloon, so thither we all troop. The Captain began by announcing to the General's chaplain that he was the Bishop of this diocese and was going to cut the ceremony short, taking the desk to emphasise his words. The Chaplain is indeed cut out of his proposed sermon, but the Captain magnanimously permits him to chime in at certain parts of the service. The little organ is ably handled by our ship's doctor. The General takes his usual place, and is a striking figure of calm dignity, with a face that grows on you, a kindly good face.

How immortally fresh and appropriate was the psalm which followed (Psa. cvii.), more especially verses 23 to 31 : " They that go down to the sea in ships and occupy their business in great waters ; these see the works of the Lord, and His wonders in the deep. For at His word the stormy wind ariseth, which lifteth up the waves thereof. They are carried up to heaven and down again to the deep ; their soul melteth away because of the trouble. They reel to and fro, and stagger like a drunken man, and are at their wits' end. So when they cry unto the Lord in their trouble He delivereth them out of their distress. For He maketh the storm to cease, so that the waves thereof are still. Then are they glad because they are at rest, and so He bringeth them to the haven where they would be. Oh that men would therefore praise the Lord for His goodness, and declare His wonders that He doeth for the children of men ! "

Then two hymns were sung, the first verse of one being especially appropriate.

FOR THOSE AT SEA.

" These men see the works of the Lord, and His wonders in the deep."

" Eternal Father, strong to save,
Whose arm hath bound the restless wave ;
Who bid'st the mighty ocean deep
Its own appointed limits keep :
    Oh hear us when we cry to Thee
    For those in peril on the sea."

I need not add that one and all were mopping

themselves, and to have heard a sermon of any length would have been insufferable, and so we bless our characteristic dismissal of said sermon. I am quite sure that the General had been told of this, for he greeted the Captain with a brilliant smile, quickly repressed, as the Captain took up his stand and in a matter-of-fact, business-like way, as much as to say, " Now it is d—d hot, and I'll have no nonsense about this, but get through as soon as possible." Strange to say, however, we all forgot the equatorial heat in our gratitude for the Lord's care of us, and in our enjoyment of the service.

There seems to be a great dark cloud of responsibility overshadowing us all, almost impossible to shake off. Little groups of officers surrounding their General and talking in undertones are frequently to be seen. As fear is unknown in the British soldier, it can but be a question of, What is best ? What is our wisest plan ? There are many officers and soldiers who have brought with them all that they hold most dear, devoted helpmeets who may have to remain in Capetown or Durban during the war.

We are all to be inoculated, it seems, in order to avoid a possible danger of typhoid. Not a pleasant thought, but as it is part of the programme, we can but submit to the inevitable.

Passing the barber's shop we find the attendant very much excited over a message from the General to the effect that he would come at twelve to get his hair cut. The barber refused every other customer for fear the General might pop in unexpectedly. Our tonsorial friend tells me afterwards enthusiastically that " the General is a gentleman, sir, and as

kind as he can be.   Just think how easily he talked
to me, yes, he did, all the time he was having his
hair cut ; and when a man came in for a pipe, and
I told him to come later, the General up and said,
' Why, give him his pipe, I am in no hurry '—and
I did."

We steam along in the most placid of waters ;

GENERAL BULLER ON HIS WAY TO THE BARBER.

only semi-occasionally does Father Neptune disturb
the deeps, as on the occasion of yesterday when we
crossed the " line," and were surprised by a visit
from the marine god and his spouse.   We noticed
one of the sailors frantically waving his hands and
shouting for the Captain to come and look.   Before
we could reach the ship's bow, which was plunging

about in rather an alarming way, we were rewarded by a curious sight, Neptune's head and shoulders in a shower of spray appearing over the bow. He held his trident in one hand while gallantly assisting his partner to climb over the rails. The couple stood in rapt wonder for a moment as Captain Rigby and his officers came forward to greet them. The august personages were immediately escorted over the ship, and for their better entertainment certain games were ordered. Two bright sailor lads quickly dropped down and went through a so-called cock-fight with their hands tied over their knees and spitted with a broom-handle. This was evidently a happy thought, as it afforded their Majesties much amusement. The purpose of the game was to try and knock each other over, using feet, elbows, and head. These events are on our Biograph, and perhaps London tastes may not be too fickle to appreciate them, considering the conditions under which these games took place ; for a sailor's life does not admit of many theatrical properties. For instance, an old rope's end is pulled apart and cut into lengths and the result is a wig.

Then we have a good game of cricket, and Father Neptune is so well pleased with his reception that he overlooks the customary tarring and feathering and final sousing and shaving of the unfortunate passenger who has no previous record for crossing the line.

Shortly afterwards we see a ship, and the log entry reads : "Sighted October 23rd, 3 p.m., the *Nineveh.*" We soon get near enough to hear the shouts of our friends, the New South Wales Lancers, *en route* to Capetown. As soon as we were near enough, Captain Rigby got General Buller up on the bridge, where he was vociferously greeted. The *Nineveh* was going much slower than our boat; the former at the rate of twelve, the latter at sixteen knots an hour, which fact allowed us to see each other but for a few short minutes.

I omitted to mention that Sunday evening, about nine, we sighted one of the Union Line boats, to which we signalled by means of a steady white light burned at the stern ; then a series of white balls of fire were thrown by rockets. The answering signal came distinctly : white light, then red rocket balls, indicating Union Line. Just then General Buller came out of his cabin rather precipitately and inquired of the Captain if any signalling were possible, but as the vessel was too far off the idea was abandoned. The General had hoped to get later news. The tidings we got at Madeira were " Kimberley surrounded, Rhodes cut off." As this Union boat had left Capetown twelve hours after the issuing of the above bulletin we all felt wild for the latest.

The crossing of the equatorial line has but one recommendation , for days wo have been feasting our eyes on indescribably beautiful sunsets. There was no heat ; on the contrary the weather was very cool, almost cold. The night before the crossing was warm, but not unpleasantly so. Nevertheless several gentlemen were seen taking up their beds and walking them on deck. This novelty was soon discontinued, however, owing to the very early swabbing of the decks and the necessity of retiring late, which admitted of but little sleep.

Wednesday, October 25th.—The ship's games have

commenced in earnest, the liveliest interest being evinced by all the classes—the second and third being admitted. The programme shows our General at the head of the committee. He is also occasionally present, showing a special interest in the tug-of-war manned by eight stalwart staff officers on one side pitted against the second-class passengers, then against the Marines. It was a magnificent sight— every muscle strained to the highest tension, and for a few moments there was no advance on either side. Gradually our friends of the staff gained a few inches in their favour, lost foot, regained, and finally, with a yell, tore along backwards, passing the knot over the chalk mark.

Thursday, 26th.—The second day of our sports opened with a dull grey sky, not photographically encouraging. At two in the afternoon we were amused with tilting at the bucket, and those who escaped a good wetting were loudly applauded. A bucket is suspended in mid-air filled with water. A board, with a hole in the middle large enough to receive the tilting-stick, is fastened to the bucket. Should the tilting-stick go through the hole, the bucket would naturally not upset, but the striking of the board upsets the balance and over goes the water on man and horse, the latter represented by a stout chap carrying his companion on his back. A good many of the passengers readily went in for these sports. The last of the series, an obstacle race, caused a great sensation.

I am now trying to get over the purgatorial pains of an inoculation against typhoid. The Staff doctor, Captain Hughes, extended to us three civilians this privilege, of which we gladly took advantage. At

five punctually we found ourselves standing in a row
meekly awaiting the execution; a hypodermic in-
jection of dead typhoid germs in your side isn't a
pleasant thought.

Friday, 27th.—What a torturous night! fever,
racking pains, and a swollen side! One of my companions has entirely collapsed, while the other one is
almost well. It is curious how much more some are
affected than others. At five this afternoon we crawl
out and dress for dinner and the fancy dress ball.
The ball is admirably got up, considering how few
things adapted to the purpose are to be found in
tightly packed steamer trunks. Sir Redvers is on
deck, laughing heartily at the costumes and the
occasionally ungainly waddle of a pair dressed as
butterflies or sylphs.

Sunday, 29th.—We are *hors de combat* through
this inoculation. At this juncture a ship hove in
sight. Great excitement ensued. General Buller,
who had quietly retired with a book newly cut for
him by Lord Gerard, popped out of his lower deck
private saloon, went to his deck cabin for glasses and
was caught, as fortunately my assistant had not left
his post. The vessel was bound for London, and
the following taken from the captain's ship's-log
reads: " Passed the *Australasia*, White Star Line, at
12.16 noon; position, 26.57 S. Latitude, 11.57 E.;
535 miles distant from Capetown." We signalled
" What news ? " and when we passed within three
hundred yards we read on a huge blackboard :

BOERS DEFEATED—THREE BATTLES—PENN-
SYMONS KILLED.

Not a shout was heard on board. The appalling

news of General Penn-Symons' death overshadowed
the good news.   Our officers only expressed the
hope that they might get a chance for vengeance.

About three o'clock, while on the bridge talking
to the officers, the look-out reported another ship in

THE GENERAL TRIED TO SHOVE THE CAPTAIN IN THE WAY.

sight. Every one rushed frantically to the sides as
the news circulated, only, however, to see a mere
speck on the horizon—evidently a ship going in the
same direction as the *Dunottar*. We quickly got
the "Bio" in position, but finding the lighting rather
poor I asked the Captain, would he change the

course of the boat, so that we should pass the steamer on our left instead of on the right ; and, as usual, he accommodatingly gave the order.   Just then Sir Redvers came tramping up the steps and gazed intently at the vessel. The camera was focussed on the General. The General tried to shove the Captain in the way, taking him by the shoulders to do so.   When I had secured three or four he called out to me : " That'll do ; if you take any more I'll throw you overboard."

Monday, October 30*th.*—We are getting out our mail-bags, 800 in number, and everybody is packing; the military cleaning up their already badly rusted swords. The Captain reports that we shall get in about eleven to-night, and hints very broadly that the General has an idea of escaping the festivities by going on shore in the tug.   I hardly think his shore friends will allow that, as a special demonstration is, we believe, in preparation.

I must close now for the mail, and if I can post anything later to catch the same mail I will do so.—Must add that we have just stopped opposite Capetown, which is brilliantly lighted.   The anchors are all out, and we sight the tug of the harbour master, Captain Stevens, coming to meet us.   I am introduced to the Captain, and he promises us his help for to-morrow.

Tuesday, October 31*st.*—Up at 5.30.   We dress rapidly while the ship is approaching the docks. We soon find ourselves surrounded by busy newsvendors.   How eagerly we read the news ; what excitement !   Soon the sun peeps out, and we rejoice in the thought of a clear day for our work. While I am busy erecting a platform opposite the

gangway through the instrumentality of the coloured
population, General Buller and his aides-de-camp
appear on deck. The General's face brilliantly
illuminated by the rays of the early sun makes us
stop and rush for our hand cameras, the result
being a series of fine pictures of the General in his
African uniform.

GENERAL BULLER AND HIS AIDES-DE-CAMP APPEAR
ON DECK.

Sharp at eight all was ready for the reception,
the machine focussed on the gangway over which
the General, his Staff, and friends were to pass,
together with General Forestier Walker, who arrived
at an early hour to breakfast with Sir Redvers.

At nine promptly the guard of honour (local

militia) presented arms while the ship's band was
playing.   Captain Rigby then bade the General

SIR REDVERS THEN PASSED ON, SALUTING A SELECT PARTY OF OFFICERS WHO CAME TO RECEIVE HIM ON BOARD.

" Goodbye."   Sir Redvers then passed on, saluting
a select party of officers who had come to receive

him on board. General Walker followed immediately behind the Captain. The guard of honour was silently and quickly inspected by Sir Redvers, who then was driven in a carriage to the Governor's house. We followed, of course.

While in town I took the first opportunity of getting acquainted with the Donald Currie Company managers, who received me most courteously, offering every assistance in their power.

We next made a visit to Cecil Rhodes' beautiful residence on the distant outskirts of the city. We arrived there in a shower of rain mixed with hail. Sir Charles Metcalf, as well as Cecil Rhodes' secretary, on whom I had counted for information, were at the seat of war. The residence in question is most picturesque, resembling in great measure the old Colonial colonnaded style; with a large porch ornamented here and there with captured Portuguese and other cannon. The house is almost obscured from view as one approaches by a beautiful grove of large evergreen trees. At the back of these trees is situated the famous menagerie. I wish I were able to describe my first sensations on touching South African soil; the overwhelming wonder of it all took possession of me afresh as I made my way to the home of this man who, more than any other, is identified with the Dark Continent. What a delight it is not to have reached that pitiable state of being *blasé*.

We have just received the news that we shall have a chance to photo the first Boer prisoners on board the *Penelope*, an old man-of-war floating prison, which necessitates our getting up at dawn in order to accomplish the task.

November 1st.—In order to facilitate our work somewhat, I decided to remain on board during the four or five days that the *Dunottar Castle* stayed in port preparatory to my leaving for Durban. Gradually the officers on board disappeared, their destination being unknown to us. All we hear is, " I am off." Some are bound for Ladysmith, others for De Aar. The last-mentioned place, we understand, will be the grand rendezvous and base of supplies, and from this point the General, we hear, will start for Kimberley to relieve Cecil Rhodes. Another report is that the General will go direct to Ladysmith. The air is full of surmise and contradiction. On Wednesday morning we arose at 5.30, and made our way as quickly as possible to the station *en route* for Simonstown, a distance of eighteen miles along the coast, where, as we were informed, the first Boer prisoners would be taken on board the prison ship *Penelope*. Arriving there, I called on Admiral Harris. He received me very kindly, but thought it would be quite impossible to get a permit from the officer in charge of the prisoners, as their orders were not to allow prisoners of war to be subjected to any indignity or annoyance. He would, however, try to get it for us.

Simonstown is very picturesque, and a good sheltered spot for the warships lying at anchor which seem to be guarding the old prison ship. We leave our Biograph outfit in charge of the good-natured dock-master, and return to Capetown, winding our way over a single track line around the numerous bays. The train at many points was almost on a level with the incoming breakers. I fancied I had had enough of the sea, but my interest was renewed at the sight of these huge waves formed, as it were, of liquid emeralds poised for a moment and then crashing at my feet.

It is still hard to realise where I am. South Africa has always seemed such an inaccessible place, full of such wonderful possibilities. It is no marvel that these colonists love the land. The Cape itself is picturesque in the extreme. Great cliffs and

SIMONSTOWN AND BAY, SHOWING BATTLESHIP "MONARCH," PRISON-SHIP
"PENELOPE," CRUISER "TERRIBLE," FLAGSHIP "DORIS."

mountains overshadow the town and surrounding villages, which in turn are often covered with clouds. A curious fact about Table Mountain is that on or about noon a white cloud is seen to slowly cover the plateau, and the people say the tablecloth is being laid for lunch. I was well pleased to have myself twice witnessed this ghost-like performance.

Thursday, November 2nd.—We are at Simonstown

again, having had to take train the night before in
order to be in time, as the prisoners were expected
to arrive at eight.   The village being overcrowded,
there was not a bed to be found for love or money,
and the night, which was bitterly cold, had to be
spent in a railway carriage.   I need not say how
glad we were to see the sun next morning.   The
warships in the bay are the following : Battleship
Monarch, prison ship *Penelope*, cruiser *Terrible*,
flagship *Doris*.   To extreme left several small gunboats are seen.   The *Penelope* shows several dents
in her sides, received in the Alexandria campaign.
Had we gone later we should have lost the *Terrible*,
which was then preparing to take Prince Christian
to Durban.   I might add that the first Boer prisoners
came on board the *Putiala*.   Rather than not get
anything of this subject we hired a boat and rowed
out to meet the launch, taking several plates with
our hand cameras while under a fire of words to
keep off.

Getting back to Capetown, we found we were
just in time to get the landing of the New South
Wales Lancers.   Through the kindness of the chief
of police we got out on to the Mayor's and County
Council's tug.   It seems that the *Nineveh* could not
dock, and it was proposed to take the Lancers off in
tugs.   Meanwhile the Mayor and his Council went
out to make them a pretty speech of welcome, after
which Captain Cox, who was in charge of the lads,
spoke for them, saying how very glad they all were
to volunteer their aid.   The Mayor remarked that
they were the first colonists who had volunteered,
and he hoped that other colonists would follow their
good example.   Captain Cox added that some of the

lads were recalled, much to their chagrin, by their parents, but he, the Captain, thought that they might remain anyhow.

On my return to shore in the Mayor's boat we quickly arranged the machine in a suitable spot, preparatory to the arrival of the Lancers, who soon rewarded us by their appearance from around the jetty in a tug picturesquely decorated with lances glistening in the sun. The boat having gone beyond the spot upon which we were focussing, and there preparing to moor, I was obliged to have the ropes thrown off, and the steamer backed into the proper place. The populace probably wondered at my cheek, but it was a success, nevertheless, for we should have failed miserably had not my good friend the chief of police furthered this move.

While the Lancers were in process of lining up and having the roll-call taken, we again removed the machine further on in order to take another view. In this process we were fairly encrusted with black savages, who fastened themselves to every available lifting part of the apparatus, yelling and screaming as they went.

Friday, November 3rd.—I devoted most of this day to the formation of our plans. Which way must we go?—that was the question. I had only this day to decide the point, as the *Dunottar* was to leave the following morning at five, and we must go on shore before six. First we took a panoramic view of the bay, then a picture of a coaling scene—a horde of black devils half naked, carrying huge sacks of coal on their backs, and performing the most extraordinary antics while screaming some wild chant to each other. The " niggers " of the Southern States are not far removed from their kith and kin over here.

At 11 a.m. I went to the Nelson Hotel to get an answer to my formal petition to follow the army. The General had told me he had no objection, but I wished to have the permission in writing. I found every one so busy that it was not until past one o'clock that I succeeded in getting at the matter. I was then told that I should receive a letter on board containing the decision.

I then asked for information regarding the army's movements, and the intelligence was such that I determined to go on with the boat to Durban, thence to Ladysmith, if possible. For us the De Aar plan would be indefinite, and perhaps fruitless, involving a wait of months ; 500 miles from here to De Aar, and another 500 to Pretoria.

Learning at the last moment that the railroads were torn up, and that we could not get through, I was forced to buy a Cape cart and harness. I had no time to buy mules or horses, so am trusting to getting them at the next stopping place, that is Port Elizabeth, the Captain promising me his help as he knows a dealer. All the carts were gone except the one we secured, which is nothing very pretty to look at, but strong and serviceable.

Sunday, November 5th.—We arrived at Port Elizabeth soon after breakfast, after twenty-eight hours of the roughest sea, which I am told is never calm at this point. As it was out of the question to sit up, we braced ourselves in our bunks and wrote up our diaries to the tune of breaking china, not far distant from our cabin. Late last night we ventured up on deck to see the brilliant phosphoric lighting

of the waves. The effect was unusually fine owing
to the turbulent state of the water. The view from
our cabin port-hole this morning was not very
enticing ; a long, low, barren strip of land, and
further on a town composed of closely packed
houses. Not far from our window, lying at anchor,
is the *Braemar Castle*, which we snap from our
port-hole.

Port Elizabeth, Monday, November 6th.—We have
packed our London box, containing notes, letters,
snap-shots, and films, and with our good angel,
Captain Rigby, we have taken a tug over to the
Tintagel Castle. We clamber over her sides and
are introduced to the captain, who listens atten-
tively to our story, and promises to see to the safety
of our packet. As he is about to weigh anchor he
is quite confident that he will be in time to catch the
mail steamer at Capetown and pass on my instructions to the next vessel.

We are then escorted over the ship to see the two
thousand refugees and their accommodation, and a
wonderful sight it is. They were packed like herrings
all over the different decks : some eating, some
sleeping, and a very few going in for a wash. The
snap-shots which we procured will give a good
idea of these irregular domestic conditions. These
wretched refugees were picked up at Natal, whither
they had flown for refuge ; but as the Government
or city authorities were unable to provide for them
they were forced to move on. Over nine hundred
were put off at Port Elizabeth, the rest distributed
along the coast towns. One snap-shot of a black
woman feeding her child is very pathetic. She has
her eyes closed, and looks the picture of weariness

and misery. From another group we pick out a baby playing with its toes on its mother's lap, while all stand around indifferent and exhausted. All

ON BOARD THE " TINTAGEL CASTLE "—A REFUGEE BLACK
WOMAN AND CHILD.

shades and classes of refugees are represented on this overcrowded boat. The Government, I believe, grants free conveyance from the seat of war south, so long as the refugees can prove that they have

friends to go to. Outside Capetown provision has
been made for them—a regular camping ground
which is said to be very comfortable. After shaking
hands with the captain of the *Tintagel Castle* we
went on shore with Captain Rigby, who was most
anxious that we should not be cheated in the
purchase of our horses. He introduced me to a
responsible dealer, and I bought a pair of fine
beasts, strong and sound. We remained two days
at Port Elizabeth, and had time to study the settlement where so many men have made their fortunes
by trading. To me it seemed inexpressibly dreary,
perhaps because we got our first impressions on a
Sunday. Monday we had an opportunity of seeing
the town, and were much surprised at the splendid
way in which the buildings were put up : no wooden
houses, all brick and stone.

Tuesday we arrived at East London, but in spite
of breakwaters it was impossible for us to land, as
the breakers were impassable, so we tossed about in
the most terrific sea for three days, unable to take
our cargo ashore. On the second day a daring tug
was seen making its way towards us, after safely
getting over the bar, near which waves were bursting
over the breakwater to the height of from 75 to
100 feet, an appalling sight. Our most daring
passengers were crowded into a long basket and
hoisted overboard, and at the proper moment when
the tug was rising on a huge wave they were instantly
lowered and bundled through a side-door. For an
hour at least this extraordinary work went on ;
every moment we feared the whole lot, tug and all,
would be swamped. The return over the bar into
the harbour was an anxious moment for all, I am

sure. Twice the tug disappeared entirely, funnel, masts, and all, and then was seen on the crest of a mountainous wave shooting forward and across the bar into the harbour.

The Captain remarked, while watching the tug's gallant tussle with the elements, " There she goes, starn up ; they'll all lose their breakfasts. Phew, there's a wallop ! Now for the bar ! Cleverly done ! Narrow run that ! "

It was heart-rending not to get a chance to biograph the waves dashing over the breakwater, but no other boat could be got to take us in and back again. No Natal passengers were allowed off, for fear that this boat might have to leave at a moment's notice and abandon the idea of landing freight.

To-day, Thursday, 9th, the weather is a little calmer, and we unload on to some lighters—a most difficult piece of work.

Before leaving this part of the world we remained up very late at night in order to see the Southern Cross, which we should hardly have recognised had it not been pointed out to us. The other false crosses look very regular, and might easily be taken for the better known " Southern Cross." It rises head down, but when at its zenith it maintains an upright position while working its way round the South Pole.

We are all curious to know what will be done at Durban with the numerous Red Cross boxes now on deck, which were put on at Elizabethport for the Boers. They will doubtless be carefully examined before being allowed to go on to these gentlemen.

At noon we left East London, after tossing around on the roughest sea I ever saw.

Friday, 10th, at 6 a.m. we arrived at Durban, one month after our departure from London, and were greeted with the news that Ladysmith was still being bombarded, that the Natal Dutch were disloyal, and that there was a possibility of the Boers coming to Durban.

A very sea-sick tug came alongside and we were lowered in a basket, spending a wretched forty-five minutes until all got safe on board. Finally the tug departs, and with many a cheer for the Captain and crew we leave the good ship *Dunottar* behind, cross the bars safely and rush through the surf, which is swarming with porpoise. The harbour reached, we pass through the Customs without difficulty, for the very simple reason that we had no baggage with us, as we intended returning for the horses, cart, and other things as soon as we had secured our rooms. Rooms, however, are not easily found. With much difficulty we secure a small one with three cots, which we gladly take as a makeshift. We are well received by the manager of Currie's Line, Mr. Wiseley, and Mr. Curry promised every assistance.

Durban, Friday, 10th.—My last notes related to our landing at Durban, and finding every corner filled, I might add a few additional details as to our house-hunting. First we tramped wearily around the place, and discovering nothing we decided to return on board, the Captain having invited us to do so if we could catch the tug; but again we were doomed to disappointment, as the last tug had left for the day, very few of them caring to venture out over the dangerously rough harbour entrance.

We again looked into the Alexander Hotel, close to the wharves, where we had been shown a large room packed with shake-down cots of indescribable hardness, but this was not to be our destiny, and we started upon another desperate search.   Hiring an exceptionally fine Zulu and his rickshaw, or hand-cart, we were pulled along, keeping our eyes open the while for the faintest sign of a bed.   Soon our horned and feathered runner lowered the shafts of our luxurious vehicle, and we were investigating the meaning of a wooden sign of " Rooms to Let."   We have since thanked Heaven for our good fortune in securing so snug a shelter.

Next morning we rose at 4.30 and made our way down to the jetty, just in time to catch the only tug going out that day to the *Dunottar Castle*.   There was not much time to lose in bringing away our horses, Cape cart, and baggage, the ship having received orders to sail at noon that day, Saturday, 11th.

The sea by this time had greatly calmed down, although not sufficiently for the tug to go alongside, and we had to go through the bar and out to sea on the huge flat-top lighters intended for the horses, which were later on securely lowered under hatches, while we found nothing but a few coils of rope to hold on to as we rolled out to sea, pitching alarm-ingly.   Soon, by a skilful turn of the rudder, the little tug succeeded in hauling our two lighters alongside the *Dunottar*, and while we were bumping about, the Captain appeared on deck in his dressing-gown, and giving us a smile of greeting, ordered a basket to be made ready and lowered for us.   By this time I was quite conscious of an indescribably disagreeable sensation, and found myself intoning dismally, " I love thee not, uncomfortable sea." But after a cold-water bath and a good breakfast I soon forgot my troubles and was discussing the latest war news with the Captain and his officers, we being the only guests on board. After breakfast the Captain insisted upon putting on his shore clothes, and after our belongings had been lowered to the lighters, we were swung out to sea in the inevitable basket, and rapidly let down to the little tug as it rose on a huge wave. We then steamed off to avoid the ship's side ; the basket, after we had been bumped on board, being released to humour the valley of water into which we quickly entered.

The approach to Durban over this truly terrifying bar of boiling, seething waves ought to deter any adventurer who has not got a good pilot on board. Added to the unrest of the water is the rather alarming aspect of the hundreds of porpoise which guard the harbour entrance, and which by the uninitiated might easily be taken for sharks. Once past the breakwaters we approach the cosy and admirably protected harbour, well patronised with various craft, ranging from large ocean steamers to gunboats, sailing vessels, and fishing smacks.

All this time my good friend, Captain Rigby, who had come purposely on shore to introduce me to his numerous friends, was delivering a most learned disquisition on the growth of Durban. Soon I was shaking hands and receiving endless promises of help from one after the other of the Captain's friends. All difficulties in the shape of Customs and stabling for the horses flew off with the gale, this while others were running around wildly, not being able to find stabling or bed, so frightfully overcrowded was the city with refugees. Noon came and the Captain returned to his vessel, having thoroughly paved the way for us.

On our return to the Customs our weapons were given back to us. These I had declared for the purpose of stamping and registration, a charge of

REFUGEE RED CROSS VOLUNTEERS GOING TO THE FRONT.

five shillings being made on each, to be refunded upon our leaving the country. Passing out of the sheds where our things had been stored, we were arrested by an extraordinary sight. Fifty or more savage-looking rickshaw-runners came racing towards us for our patronage, each one more grotesquely decorated than the other — horned, winged, feathered, and dressed in every conceiv-

4

able garb to attract the visitor. This attire was set off by fiendish yells and capers, and I felt that in all my travels I had never seen anything so unique.

Picking out a veritable Umslopogas worthy of Rider Haggard fame, we sat watching and wondering at the perfect symmetry and development of these magnificent specimens of manhood—an attractive race, cleanly in body and habit, pure-minded, moral people. I can find nothing but good spoken of the Zulu, and the kindliest things said of the Kaffir who swarm all over Natal.

That night we slept the sleep of the just, and rose much refreshed.

Sunday, 12th.—At 5 a.m. we found ourselves on the wharf prepared for action, having learned late the night before that the *Roslin Castle,* filled with troops, would be in at 6 a.m.; so, with the assistance of twelve turbaned chaps, we had our flat waggon wheeled into position and all got in readiness. Not until nine, however, were we rewarded by a sight of the ship, crowded from one end to the other and far up into the rigging with khaki-coloured uniforms and helmets. Eleven hundred troopers and ninety officers all told. No words can ever describe the thrill of the moment, as the huge vessel slowly and majestically rounded the wharf and was gently drawn in amidst the deafening hurrahs of the thousands on the shore and on the surrounding decks of the harbour boats. We were busy with a vengeance, all our cameras at work, and before the day was out and the troops gone we had many pictures, covering the various scenes enacted that sunny, happy Sunday, when the faithful and loyal people of Durban rejoiced and their anxieties passed away. To add to their joy a message was received from General Buller to the people of Durban and Natal, highly commending them for their fidelity and loyalty. The General is still quietly at Cape-town, and if we had remained, our days would have been wasted, whereas now we are making every preparation to get away toward the seat of war.

THE " ROSLIN CASTLE " ARRIVING AT DURBAN.

Among the snap-shots taken on this eventful Sunday will be found several views of the *Roslin Castle's* approach to the pier, showing a mass of helmeted troopers hanging over the sides, many having clambered up the riggings. After the landing, some of the snaps showed Colonel Kitchener talking to one of his officers. The rest were views of the stacked accoutrements of the troops ; " A First Meal on Shore " ; a general view of the men preparing to board the waiting railroad cars ; " Getting in," " The Departure," " A Thirsty Man," &c.

The Biograph pictures are historically consecutive, from the landing of the troops to the departure of the last train containing a few cars loaded with the Medical Staff, stretcher-bearers, and Hospital Corps. This was not the largest train-load by any means, but certainly the most important that day. In one of the Biograph series a group of the Castle Line managers is conspicuous in the foreground, reading Chamberlain's speech of the 20th in the *Times*.

Monday, 13th, was a day set apart to prepare our-selves for a plunge into the interior, and it was as much as we could do to keep on our feet, as we were driven here and there by the terrific wind-storm, which carried clouds of fine sand through the air. Both cart and horses were overhauled, and a list of necessary articles decided on. All our luggage had to be left behind, with the exception of absolutely indispensable things. A tent to cover our cart, ex-tending over the shaft and closed at both ends so as to keep all dry and cool, had to be planned and made. Cooking utensils, eatables, and other neces-saries had to be collected before we could say " Trek away." We fastened the Biograph to the back seat, so as to be able to fire at a moment's notice, the whole to be elevated or lowered at will from the pole, or cart-shaft. This waggon will have to be our hotel for some time to come, so we try to make our arrangements as simple and practical as possible. We are told that intense heat and bitter cold, with much rain, may be expected higher up.

Tuesday, 15th.—The *Spartan* hospital ship next has our attention, and many good snaps are secured, showing the wards, &c. ; also the convalescents on deck, who greet us with marvellous tales of hairbreadth escapes. One man was shot through his

COLONEL KITCHENER AND ONE OF HIS OFFICERS.

helmet, the ball just skinning the head and rendering the man unconscious for hours.

Wednesday, 15th.—Rain, rain, rain, so we continue our preparations for the great trek, arranging also for the transport of our cart and horses, a very difficult matter as all the railroads are under military control. However, after explaining the purport of our trip to

Mr. David Hunter, General Manager, Natal Government Railway, that gentleman acceded most graciously to all my wishes, namely to give us all railway facilities as well as transport for our cart and horses. It was therefore arranged that whenever we could not go any further by train, we would drive to the next spot of unbroken rail.

Another big load of soldiers came in to-day and the docks and railways are kept busy, the people of Natal never seeming tired of the sight and shouting themselves hoarse with delight. Durban is overwhelmingly happy. Troops by the thousand are pouring in daily and the warships are ready for action. Each morning the marines from the man-of-war *Terrible* may be seen near the town hall, drilling round their cannons, which are painted khaki colour, and which were brought on shore the day we arrived. As the rumour gained ground that the Boers were coming, many prominent men in the city fortified their homes. It is quite a sight to see Captain Scott and his marines at cannon drill. No finer set of chaps have I ever seen, formidable in appearance, with their belts crowded with cartridges, pulling a hundred strong on the ropes, and dragging the 4.7 guns through the street. As soon as Captain Scott of the *Terrible*, who commands here, was disengaged, I asked him if he had anything for me from the War Office, but not having yet received the cablegram, I suppose I am to wait patiently. I explained the object of my visit and what I intended to do. I found it difficult to keep from laughing while talking to the Captain when I thought of the absurdly funny way he was locked up by the wharf and river police for being out later than 11 p.m.

last night. All his explanations were of no avail. He stated that he was the Commander, and that he himself it was who had made this regulation. At the police-station he again made the statement, but was locked up, and had to send for an officer to identify him before he was released.

Thursday, 16th.—The *Armenian* has just come in with 604 horses, eighteen guns, and 900 men, cavalry and artillery. Great excitement prevails, while the cars on the landing are being loaded up with guns and horses, which are slung out of the ship and lowered on the wharf and cars. A Biograph picture shows a train-load of these guns *en route* for Estcourt, drawing into Durban station from the Point (where they have been loaded). The guns are all painted khaki colour, a dirty, yellow, earthy shade. In less than twelve hours every horse had been sent to the front, and until a late hour we could hear from our windows the cheers of the soldiers and people, to the snorting accompaniment of a pair of overloaded engines.

The tent is ready, the stallions less restive, and possibly we can get away Saturday morning. The railroad company here has promised me every facility so far as it is concerned, but I may come up against a military brick wall, which I suppose I must work through.

An armoured train is reported to be going up to Estcourt, and we hitch up our restive beasts to our Cape cart and plunge through the streets, scattering rickshaws, Zulus, Kaffirs, Arabs, &c., amid a chorus of yells. The scene reminded me forcibly of a swarm of black cockroaches, rudely surprised during a feast. We arrived just too late to secure the view, and I had

to arrange, not without considerable difficulty, to get
the scene for next day, for which facility we were
indebted to the courtesy of both the railroad managers
and the officers in charge.

Our stallions meanwhile had very much alarmed
the natives (who were hanging around the cart) by
their antics, standing on their hind-legs and coolly
taking little lumps out of each other.   My assistant,
Mr. Cox, had been using various mild persuasions,
but these proving ineffectual I gave them a sound
thrashing.   They had tasted blood, however, and I
found it difficult to dissuade them from finishing
their meal.   The price of the old whip and the new
one got them O.K., and soon they were trotting
amicably side by side, well matched in colour and
gait.   They are a delight when at peace with each
other, but what a time we have to hitch up !   The
beasts are led out daily with the utmost caution, the
process of hitching taking all three of us to accomplish.   I have had to put a nose-bar between them
to prevent their getting their heads together.   Even
this doesn't always answer, so I station my assistants
at their heads while I get hold of the reins ; and
when a brief interval occurs between frolics, plung-
ings, and bitings, they let go and we are off, my
nimble companions scrambling in behind as best they
can.   I hope this superfluous energy will resolve
itself into good hard pulling, for the brutes are very
strong, and when at peace pull well together.   They
were the best I could get in Port Elizabeth, the
other creatures being in a pitiable state of decline.

At 6.30 each morning we have a little circus ring
on the beach in which to exercise our beasts, in
which sport we ourselves get a good share by whip-

ping them around and round in a circle until they
get less frisky. Then we hitch them under the usual
restrictions.

Before closing the day, I must mention how terri-
fied our rickshaw runners are of being caught out a
single moment after 11 p.m. At 10.30 we left the
Royal Hotel, where we called for news from our
friends, and tried to induce several runners who
were hurrying in, to take us to our rooms, but for
answer they scurried past with frightened looks,
only shaking their horned heads at us. It became
imperatively necessary for us to get indoors, and by
running we knew we could do so and be in regulation
time ; so catching a feathered Zulu twice my strength
and swallowing capacity, I forced him to run us.
Never shall I forget that " run " to my dying day.
We were off like a shot, swiftly and silently—a horse
could not have gone any faster. With perspiration
rolling off his huge muscular, bare back, his chest
rising and falling in perfect rhythm with the felt-
like patter of his feet, he sped along encouraged by
voice and an occasional peep at a half-crown, at which
he covetously took time to give a sideway glance,
thus affording me an opportunity to get a glimpse
of his fine and noble features. He was a veritable
Umslopogas. This, of course, vividly recalls Rider
Haggard's masterly description of the death-ride of
Umslopogas for the White Queen. For fear the
fellow might be caught I sent him back when within
easy distance of our quarters, much to his delight.
He raised his hand high above his head on receiving
the money, crying, " Baba, baba dank." Then away
at double pace he went, relieved of his load.

Friday, 17*th*.—We visit the refugee settlement and

plan for a Biograph picture in the event of our not being able to get away to-morrow. Every available space was taken up by the refugees, tents everywhere, hundreds preparing their meals. Those who were unable to get tents sleep in the great town drill-halls in carts, and appear wonderfully comfortable.

At 10.30 we were on the spot, ready for the picture of the armoured train which was in preparation for its run to the front, carrying food for the army. In spite of the slight rain and rather discouraging aspect of the weather from a photographic standpoint, all went off as we had desired. Everything was painted khaki colour; we hope it will all come out well. I was fortunate in being able to include in the picture the managerial staff, Mr. David Hunter and others, as they watched the armoured train slowly leaving Durban. We hope it will have better luck than the last two trains sent out. The first engine fortunately escaped being derailed yesterday at Estcourt, and dashed through last night to Durban in time for the Biograph picture. What luck! The tender shows fifty or more heavy dents made by the Boer Mauser bullets; a close snap-shot taken before the departure may show the indentations. It will be of interest to note that the armoured train has two engines, one in the middle and one in front; the one in front was put on especially for me owing to its history and yesterday's narrow escape. It will be switched off at next station.

Saturday, 18th.—Still in Durban, hoping to get some other war scenes, but after waiting two extra days we have decided to leave Monday for Pietermaritzburg.

ARMOURED TRAIN LEAVING DURBAN.

Sunday morning (19*th*) we went for our salt bath, which might more properly have been called a sand bath, owing to the furious wind storm which pelted us on the beach. The only way by which we could keep our khakis and helmets from blowing away was to deposit them in big holes which we dug in the sand. While dodging breakers and jelly-fish, &c., we noticed a large ship steaming in among the men-of-war stationed without our harbour. It proved to be the *Armenian*, a huge boat loaded with troopers, cavalry and artillery. The day not being suitable for picture-taking, and besides as we had so many views of this kind, we made no attempt to secure a photo of it. Troops are of course pouring in now day and night.

Monday morning.—We harnessed our restive beasts and busied ourselves collecting our effects. We first stored our personal luggage in the R.R. station, and having received an invitation to visit the Hon. Mr. Jameson's home, seven miles outside Durban, we dashed out in less than an hour through an indescribably interesting country, peopled with Kaffirs, Zulus, and many other odd and picturesque specimens of humanity. We found the country exceedingly beautiful, mountainous and thickly overgrown with luxuriant trees and bushes, nearly all new to me; dotted here and there with huge century plants and palms.

We received from Mr. Jameson, his wife and family, a genuine Scotch welcome. They seemed kindly anxious to make us forget that we were so far away from home, entertaining us for the pleasant two hours of our stay with wondrous tales of their pioneering days. They conducted us through their enchanted grounds, rich with endless varieties of tropical growth. Mr. Jameson is a very fine botanist, and has been remarkably successful in growing his collection of tropical plants, which include wonderful specimens of the bottle and screw palms. The rich and delicate gradation of colour seen in his grouping of the flowering trees and shrubs is very striking. After a fragrant cup of tea under the scarlet flowering umbrella tree, our hosts conducted us into a native kraal made of bamboo grass and palm-leaves, shaped like an inverted bowl, lighted only from the entrance, three feet wide. The fireplace is in the centre, and the smoke rising, filters out through the bamboo and loose covering, which, curiously enough, does not allow the rain to penetrate. A Kaffir, I was told, is proverbially hospitable, and should a traveller desire to rest a while among Kaffirs, he need only seek the chief and simply inform him of his intention to remain awhile among them, and immediately a hut is cleaned out, or a new one built and put at his disposal. The traveller, however, must speak the language and entertain his host with the news of the day, that being the only compensation asked. There is something so naïve and childlike in the Kaffirs that you get to love them as you would a big dog; in many ways they remind one of the good old-fashioned, unspoiled plantation negro of the Southern States of America.

Before leaving we were given a sight of the surrounding country from the verandah, and found it surpassingly beautiful and wildly picturesque, surrounded on three sides by mountains thick with trees. All this section was, until very recently,

crowded with elephants and wild beasts. Mrs.
Jameson remarked, " They frequently called on us
when we first came here, the elephants rubbing up
against our flimsy structure, threatening to crush it
in, greatly to our alarm. They are plentiful even
now, and may be seen in the valley going to water
at the river glistening far down there at our feet."
How vividly Rider Haggard's descriptions of South
African life came before me as I greedily drank in all
I saw and heard.

At last we had to terminate our visit and leave
most regretfully this little paradise, to again pursue
our way into unknown and possibly dangerous
fields.

On our way back to the hotel we visited a Hindoo
temple, and, much to our inconvenience, were called
on to take off our riding-boots before being permitted
to enter even the antechamber, beyond which we
could see the Hindoo gods, grotesquely hideous,
grinning at us in our discomfiture. One of my
companions pointed out two bottles within easy
reach of one of the green-eyed gods, which looked
suspiciously like beer or wine, although presumably
oil to fill the ever burning lamps, several of which
were hanging around. A few of the gods, as we
noticed on our way out, had been ruthlessly deprived
of heads and legs and cast aside in the grass, others
better looking having taken their place.

Monday, 20th.—We leave Durban, and through
the courtesy of Mr. David Hunter we, together with
our horses, cart, and baggage, are to be conveyed
free throughout Natal. By this means we shall be
enabled to use the lines whenever unbroken. Just
as we are about to leave, the popular stationmaster,

Mr. Irons, reports that all communication is cut off to Estcourt, so we decide to go to Pietermaritzburg and wait our chances. At 10.15 we are off, and are rushed along through the mountains on a well-bedded single track road, running smoothly as it glides along endless curves in and out among the hills. We dare not close our eyes, for fear of losing any new or interesting sight. Besides the fine scenery we were much entertained by the funny little huts of every description around which groups of half-naked Kaffir families were seen variously unoccupied, for they never seemed to worry themselves about work unless when goaded by song and gesture. We saw them later on lifting heavy rails, about fifty men to a rail. This scene I must try and biograph before leaving Africa.

At 3.10 we reached Pietermaritzburg, capital of Natal, and found the station overcrowded with soldiers and luggage. After some hours we got our effects stored in a corner, and kept our eyes and ears open for news. Our waiting was not for long. A train from the direction of Hanover brought us a bedraggled, worn-out half-dozen troopers and their horses, under command of our friend, Captain Kayser, who was on board the steamship *Dunottar Castle*. An attempt had been made to signal to Ladysmith heliographically. The party, under the guidance of two mountain police or guides, left Estcourt Thursday, the 16th, and after hard riding got halfway to Ladysmith, when one of the men, using his opera glass, discovered Boers on a very distant hill; but as no one else saw them it was thought to be a mistake, and the party went on—soon, however, to discover five hundred Boers making for

them. Some Kaffirs (who are said to be our best
friends here) hid the troopers' horses in a kraal
while our men lay low between hillocks. The
narrator, while describing his sensations when the
Boers scampered by, remarked that he nearly choked
for fear they would hear him breathe. They were
desperately anxious to push on to signalling distance.

AN ATTEMPT IS MADE TO SIGNAL HELIOGRAPHICALLY TO LADYSMITH.

The present danger over, the party recovered their
horses, but owing to continued cloudy weather the
heliograph signalling instrument could not be put to
any use that time, and a *détour* of nearly two hundred
miles had to be made before getting to the railroad
near Pietermaritzburg, where we met them on their
arrival.

Monday night we found the city so frightfully overcrowded that we had to sleep on sofas in a miserable parlour of a tenth-rate despicable inn. What a night!

Next day, Tuesday, we pitched our tent in a beautiful field near the railroad station, yet not too near to be deprived of sleep by the ceaseless going and coming of the trains bearing our troops. We face the mountains and lovely valley, our horses grazing near by in charge of a Kaffir all ready for a run should a call come, such as "Troops coming!" Up we jump! Hitch up! and away we dash!—our camera, a fixture on the back seat, being always in readiness. This arrangement of camera is admirably adapted to our requirements owing to the difficulty—in fact impossibility—of getting conveyances or help. Every one is busy with troops, carting ammunition, procuring horses and mules for shipment. The work here is well-nigh indescribable, though I will endeavour by next mail to say something about it. We are sending our first Bio picture of a train-load of troops for Mooi River. Estcourt cut off. Cannot proceed yet.

Monday, November 27th, Pietermaritzburg.—We are now pulling up stakes to make for Estcourt, having received from General Buller all necessary papers to proceed to wherever I wish; this is the result of a personal petition to Sir Redvers, a clause in the papers reading that I be permitted to accompany troops in the field. So we load up our things on the cart and drive to the R.R. station. We put cart and horses on a truck placed at our service by the kindness of the general manager of the line, Mr. Hunter, then proceed with the 3.10. On reaching

Highland station we photographed the wrecked safe lying on the platform, and heard the story over again from the stationmaster of how the Boers destroyed everything they could lay their hands on.

We arrived at Mooi River station at about 7 o'clock, and were quietly told we could not go any further that night, as they feared the track had been tampered with. So we crawled out, and made the best of it by arranging to stay all night at the little railroad station inn. Supper came first, then bed, if either can be so called. The wretchedly nervous landlady, assisted by her black servitors, Indian and Kaffir, did their best for the belated travellers. After a severe tussle with some leathery beef and other indestructibles, we sought our bunks, not, however, until I made my peace with the landlady (with whom we had some differences owing to the bad accommodation of her inn). I heard from her a pitiful story of her troubles. The Boers, after shelling the place, drove her out and took possession, but they were not allowed to remain very long, as our men cleared them off the night preceding our arrival, when she was reinstated. After hearing all this a feeling of rather belated thankfulness came over me for the meal we had consumed. It was food, after all.

Tuesday, 28th.—We are shaken up by our amiable stationmaster to catch the 5.30, and, floundering into the kitchen, drink a cup of scalding tea to keep out the cold. The nights here grow bitterly cold towards morning. Just as we are leaving we are greeted by a curious sight; hundreds of soldiers black as ink are disembarking from open railroad trucks, to camp a few hours. They eat their breakfasts standing. They were simply unrecognisable from the smoke and dust of the locomotive, but not a complaint did I hear; all cheery and in good spirits—brave chaps! They laughingly submitted to being photographed, which was a rather longer process than usual, owing to the early and therefore weak morning light.

Estcourt.—The Boers were made to vacate the place a few days ago, and were driven further up the line. The place is in a terrible state of confusion, troops packing up and R.R. station crowded. After spending a few hours in getting my papers countersigned, and snap-shotting everything of interest, I decided to take the first train on to the end of the road, *i.e.* Frere, the Boers having blown up the bridge there and stopped traffic. We were permitted to go on the open train, which was loaded down with ammunition and food, guarded by the marines of H.M.S. *Terrible,* accompanying their huge guns. It was an exciting ride; a photo shows where and how we were seated while feeling our way along, expecting at every turn of the road to be derailed or *potted* at! Strangely exhilarating!

Suddenly as we came up over a hill, two men were seen madly waving a flag, with diagonal black streak, pointing at us, then suddenly disappearing. This had the opposite effect of calming us, especially as an officer seated at my side on a box of cartridges ominously remarked, "There are a lot of men going over that hill—look!" They were too distant, however, for us to distinguish their uniforms, but in order to keep up the excitement we preferred, of course, to believe they were hostile; and up to date we are still uncertain.

A marvellous sight greeted us on approaching Frere; tents and soldiers on every hand as far as the eye could reach. We rushed rapidly along into the station, which was full of soldiers in khaki and helmets, standing ready to assist in unloading the big guns, ammunition, and provisions which had been so fortunate as to escape the enemy.

ENTRAINING WOUNDED AT CHIEVELEY STATION.

In spite of the general activity we succeeded in getting the use of an engine and flat car, and in taking a Biograph panorama run of the camp. In this undertaking we were materially assisted by the courteous and capable stationmaster. The public must not too severely judge this picture, as the goods van, or flat car, lacked the best of springs, and consequently the scene might show considerable vibration. Owing to the impossibility of getting our cart and tent, the gunners being busy all the afternoon unloading the guns, we were obliged to sleep in a car which we were fortunate enough to find on a siding. There we cooked our desultory meal on an oil-stove, and proceeded to make the best of the night. The stationmaster joined us at my invitation, and although we had no course dinner or champagne, he swore that he hadn't enjoyed a dinner so much for weeks. " Food is so scarce," he remarked, " that I am hungry all the time, and cannot even get leisure to eat what there is." This was our menu : cocoa, bread and cheese, and canned figs—not a sumptuous repast. The stationmaster dilated upon the chronic activity of things. " Trains with troops and goods trains are constantly coming in," he said ; " I haven't a bed even, only a shake-down in the depôt. I had to give up my house over there," pointing to a pretty stone building, " to General Hildyard and Staff. They are welcome to that and everything I have, if they will only get square on those butchers who looted my house and tore everything to pieces."

Wednesday, 29th.—We wake at dawn to the clash of shunting trains. Breakfast over, we toil at the unloading of our Cape cart and goods in order to take a view of the broken bridge, and the reconstruction of the same. Our Biograph is carried down to the stream facing the bridge, and I get a good view of the new foundation laid for the wooden trestles. The Kaffirs as help are simply invaluable, and they may be seen and heard everywhere as they cheerfully toil, chanting the while keeping time with

their work. Every hand stopped work and gazed
steadily at the camera while taking the first picture,
thus depriving us of the necessary movement. After
this we had of course to make another attempt. I
learned that every bridge in Natal has a duplicate
ready to be erected, and as soon as the Frere bridge
had been blown up the authorities telegraphed to

REPAIRING THE RAILROAD.
KAFFIRS AT WORK, CHANTING THE WHILE.

Durban for another. Meanwhile this wooden trestle-
bridge is being rapidly built in order to pass over the
troops and guns, &c., to Colenso. Our camp was
pitched at last, and only just in time to keep the
floor dry, as a furious rain and wind storm burst
upon us. All hands were called on to help hold
the tent down, and soon we were dripping wet

while battling with the elements to prevent the whole camp from sailing heavenwards. The storms in Natal are frequent and severe, and as we have just arrived in time for them, we must submit, I suppose, and try to enjoy them if possible.

We are comfortably ensconced a few feet above the riverside, and are lulled to sleep by the sound of the rushing stream and bellowing cattle. Horses, oxen, cows, sheep, and goats, all are driven into a large kraal or enclosure from the surrounding hills, and find room in our midst. Our boys do not seem to mind these little marauding expeditions, and invariably return with great numbers of these animals, not deeming it necessary to consult Mr. Boer anent the same.

Not five miles away the Boers are camped, and all day yesterday we were hearing from them. Lady-smith's guns are plainly audible, and last night and to-night the sky has been streaked with searchlights projected on the clouds from both Estcourt and our Frere camp in order to get in touch with Ladysmith, all telegraphic communication having been cut off for some time past. We hope soon to see an answering searchlight ticking off dots and dashes in reply. The effect is magical. There cannot, I should think, be any doubt about these messages reaching Ladysmith. Late into the night the signals were kept up, and I found it difficult to keep from watching and trying to decipher the messages, which of course it was impossible to do, as they were in code. Coming up from Mooi River on top of the ammunition and gun train, I had a good opportunity of studying the lay of the land. Innu-merable stone works and shelters could be seen in every direction. I made a rough sketch at the time, which may be of interest. Huge boulders are rolled together and form a good shelter from bullets, although I am told that much danger is encountered from broken chips of rock and pebbles.

Frere Camp, December 3rd.—I gave but a meagre account of my visit to the wrecked armour train, owing to the immediate necessity of sending the packet off to Maritzburg. It was intended by the Boers to derail the train down into the stream, but owing to the impetus it dragged on for over three hundred yards, and then went over the embankment assisted by the shelling. The derailing, as is now well known, was effected by filling in between the inner rail and guide rail, using an extra length of rail and stones. If they had simply put the smallest series of obstruction on the upper rail, where nearly the whole weight of the train was bearing, the entire train would have gone crash down into the stream, as was the intention of the Boers. We drove out to the spot hoping to get a picture with the armoured train in the background, but found it impossible to arrange at that time.

We came across the grave of one of the victims of the disaster, marked with stones " R.D.F., A.C.Co.—Pray for our comrades "; and took a snap-shot of the scene while some soldiers were looking at the grave with helmets off. Further on we came to the wreck, close to which we found another grave. Two soldiers were working on the inscription, while several of their comrades were watching them in silence. I learned that there were five lads buried here, and that one or two had not yet been accounted for. On questioning the soldiers camped round the spot, I ascertained that if I crawled far in under one of the huge cars I could feel a leather strap caught under the *débris*, and presumably attached to some unfortunate soldier. I did so, and with a crowbar dug around the tip of the strap, and succeeded after half an hour's work in getting the two scraps out. It was a difficult undertaking, for I was almost overpowered by the strong odour. I then called for some volunteers to help dig around in the hope of being able to get at the remainder of the strap, and what might be attached to it; but we only succeeded in digging out a large number of cartridges, scraps of shell, and a soldier's kit knife, &c.

Before we left the lads served out tea, as we didn't dare to drink the water, and entertained us with yarns of the goriest nature. Returning across the veldt, we stopped for a moment to sympathise with a native whose house had been burned, effects looted, and cattle carried off.

Wending our way through the beautiful hills and dales, we saw a charming cottage far down in the hollow, and were enticed to pick our way along the ravine avoiding the thousands of ant hills, in order to find out some war news from the inmates. We soon discovered that the house was deserted, the sole inhabitant greeting us with a pitiably hungry purr. I cannot hope to describe the wretched condition of everything inside, a general smash-up; pictures, books, photograph albums, letters, &c., all scattered about, and torn and trampled; cupboards and bedsteads upside down, and in fact the home ruined. My companion, curiously enough, picked up a label traceable to one of his relatives, addressed to this once happy home.

Many more of such scenes did we witness, but
as time is too short to do more than touch upon
this one example, we must drive on and meet the
returning cavalry, who were called upon this afternoon to repel the Boers from our outposts. About
3 p.m. three distant cannon-shots were heard. Instantly the bugles called to horse, and five hundred
strong galloped away before we could intercept
their path with our Biograph. The Boers had
disappeared, and our boys returned shortly before
six by another road or track, a formidable lot, well
mounted and in the best of spirits, though " damn
sorry we didn't get a whack at the pigs. But better
luck next time ; we'll give them a chance yet to
remember our mugs." Then spying the Biograph,
" Here, Jimmy, come and see your face. Why,
here's a looking-glass in this here machine wot you
call movin' picters." His companions crowded
around, making each in turn the most absurd
remarks as they looked at their own unshaven and
sunburnt faces in the mirror of our finder. " Just
look at that, will yer ! " " What would Sal think of
me now ? " and so on.

Our camp is pitched on the side of an almost dry
stream, which our friends the Royal Engineers are
damming up to supply the various camps with
water. Hundreds of sandbags are thrown together,
bridging the stream in order to raise the water
three or four feet higher. If this water were to be
cut off by the Boers, or the stream dry up, Frere
Camp would be in a sore plight.

A snap-shot shows the Royal Engineers hard at
work. The whole stream is graded in its useful-
ness ; the first and upper part is for drinking

purposes, the second is given over to the cattle and horses, and below the road, near the blown-up bridge, hundreds of soldiers may be seen at all hours bathing.

Frere Camp, December 4th.—We saddled up and visited the outposts, going from hill to hill within sight of the Boers, who are comfortably ensconced

W. K.-L. Dickson.   Wm. Cox.

INTERIOR BIOGRAPH TENT AT FRERE CAMP, DEC. 4TH, 1899.

three miles off, at the foot of the great blue hills, with Umbulutana Mountain prominent. We searched the plain in front of the hills with our glasses, and ascertained that, although mere specks, they were Boers. This was our first sight of the great camp of over 15,000 men.

We proceeded to some of the entrenched guns, and had it been possible to haul our heavy apparatus up the hill, we could have secured most valuable pictures of firing on the Boers who had overstepped the line and were trying to get at Chieveley station, indicated at the right of our rough sketch. The guns are those used on board H.M.S. *Terrible*, twelve-pounders. The larger guns are now half-way to our outposts ; forty-pounders are also being prepared, all these being got into position at night so as to prevent the Boers from studying our defences. It might be interesting to add that the twelve-pounders do deadly work at five miles, and the forty-pounders at ten miles.

We may yet be able, by the assistance of the soldiers, to carry our fiery apparatus to the hill-tops during the night, but as we cannot tell just when the guns will be used, our machine may have to remain up there for days.

Tuesday, December 5th.—We drove out to the outposts again in search of Bio views, for as yet the bridge at Frere is not ready, and no trains can go over. Moreover, no orders have been issued from General Buller to advance. We stopped at a looted Boer farm, once a comfortable and beautiful homestead, and made the best of it. Some of the soldiers made tea for us, catching the rainwater in pans, a sharp storm having risen while we were there. It would be impossible to describe the chaotic condition of the farm. It was our people this time ; they smashed everything and commandeered the cattle, five hundred strong, which we had photographed the day before. Our people discovered that the four sons of the house had joined the enemy, and they being disloyal nothing could save it. Absolute ruin ensued, and the mother and younger children were sent off the premises. It was also ascertained that one of the sons was a clever photographer, and had secured a large number of negatives and prints of every rail-road bridge in Natal. These our people promptly appropriated. In view of our long trip back, we contented ourselves with some hurried photographs of the interior and drove off.

SIGNALLING TO LADYSMITH AND SHELLING BOER POSITIONS AT MIDNIGHT.

That night, at the invitation of the naval officers, I visited the searchlight signal station, an impromptu and most ingenious construction. Through the help of Mr. David Hunter, our naval friends of H.M.S. *Terrible* succeeded in putting together a boiler engine and dynamo on a flat car, shielded by iron sheets; one of the searchlights of the *Terrible* was put in operation on another car. The signalling apparatus of a multiple-slot shutter, operated by a lever, cut off or turned on the rays at will, which threw out a beam of light of great brilliancy, clearly discernible in the sky, especially when projected on a cloud. These signals are to be read by our unfortunate Ladysmith prisoners, who have been trying to answer our messages with a feeble flash machine, only visible to our night outposts. This outfit travels up and down the line, and was at first stationed at Estcourt, but is at present established at Frere. This signal station on wheels is constructed and put into operation in thirty-six hours.

Wednesday, December 6th.—Took snap-shots of camp life in the morning, then drove out again to the scene of the armoured train disaster, intent upon taking a Bio view of the grave of those who perished at that time.

December 7th.—We again visited the outposts, and managed, not without extreme difficulty, to haul our machine, &c., to the top of Rifle Hill signal station, just in time to catch a message from Colonel Kitchener, which was flagged to picket No. 8, the operators kindly waiting until we got the machine in position before they sent the message. The men were watching the enemy below while the signalling was in progress, Captain Bartram being in command of signal and picket. This is a splendid scene, and one of which we are very proud, for we nearly killed ourselves and our horses in our endeavour to get planted in time. We could not have secured it but for the extreme courtesy of the officer. This is the message which was sent to O. C. No. 8 picket : "Have your picket under arms and send out patrol. Kitchener, December 7th."

It was sent in plain flag, Morse, not code, so that any one who knew Morse could read this message.

We can get no help at all, Coolie or Kaffir, and rarely a soldier can lend any aid unless I go to about fifteen officers and generals, running the gauntlet of the usual red-tape. Rather mixed metaphor, but no matter; really, come to think of it, nothing matters much these days.

RIFLE HILL SIGNAL STATION.

There is ample work for my small staff. It takes half our time to get grub and water and to pitch our tent, besides caring for our horses; the poor beasts seem to be growing thinner daily, the result, we fear, partly of occasionally getting away and eating wet grass. It is called "horse sickness." If the horses fail, we fail.

One military officer high in authority has done

everything to block my path, and to prevent the world from seeing these views. I have yet to discover his motive. On board the steamship *Dunottar* I handed him my card and requested him to make an appointment for me to see Sir Redvers Buller. He promised to do so. The days passed, however, without his having redeemed his promise. I then hunted him up again, and found he had done absolutely nothing. I then determined to interview the General myself, and found him entirely satisfactory, notwithstanding his chronic dislike to being photographed. It was at this interview that I obtained from him the promise of a field pass. I got no other opportunity of seeing him before landing, to secure the pass, but knowing I should obtain it later on, I pushed on from Capetown to Durban and on to Maritzburg, as above stated. After many another unaccountable attempt on the part of this same high official to prevent my obtaining General Buller's pass, I finally succeeded in obtaining it from Sir Redvers personally; and it is amazing to relate that so virulent was this official's objection to yielding to even General Buller's permit for my accompanying the army, that he issued an order that I should draw no rations for myself, men, or horses, knowing that this would in all probability prevent my proceeding with the army. But it didn't, though he also ordered that we should be thrown out of camp if we persisted in following. The upshot of the whole is that two hours after hearing of this inexplicable order I pulled up pegs and marched forward. We were stopped at Estcourt, and while I was foraging for food was handed a note reading, " Tell Mr. Dickson I expressly forbid his going on.

Send him back with his men. (Signed) ———," indirectly from the aforesaid high official. I only
laughed to myself, still feeling secure with the
General's permit. My papers were overhauled, some
surprise evinced during the examination, and then a
muttered apology. I reached the station and was
preparing to go, when again I was stopped by the
query: "Where was my pass between stations?" I
had the general pass, but not the detail local one
from station to station. All my papers were collared,
and I finally had to send my friend Seward for them.
At Frere I found I could not do without horse food.
We had tinned stuff. Rather than give up I have
run back on the line for food, and still am free.

December 8th.—To-day we moved up to the very
outposts with the naval brigade and their big guns,
hoping to be able to follow them to the front. They
were extremely kind and helpful. My message to
Captain Jones, the chief, received a most courteous
reply, with the information that he would be glad to
help me. Commander Limpus gave me every assistance in our first picture, the subject of which was
their pitching camp. All promised to help me get a
picture of the firing on the enemy. I am now sending this and the few films and snaps before crossing
the lines, for fear our cart may get taken, and, in
fact, we ourselves be made prisoners. I have only
touched lightly upon my many troubles. Nothing
could give an idea of how I have been bothered and
annoyed despite the ægis of General Buller's protection. Of course nothing could save me from the
incubus of a very caravan of an outfit, a broiling sun
all day, bitterly cold nights, only canned food, and
no bread for days.

To-night we push on in the dark, not a light allowed. It is quite possible we may land in some ravine. I shall chance it, and possible capture.

Outposts between Frere and Chieveley, December 8th.—Finding that we should have to conform to certain rather harassing rules and regulations should we join the correspondents and depend on getting pictures from information of movements, &c., I decided to make the acquaintance of some of the generals and colonels connected with the various brigades, regiments, &c., so I finally joined the naval division under command of Captain Jones and Commander Limpus, who courteously invited us to their camp, and thereafter afforded us every desirable facility. After rapid preparation we followed them to their outposts, which were some five miles in advance of where we then were, that is, at the general camp.

At midday we had to lunch under the shadow of the Biograph, whose huge proportions afforded great relief from the broiling, fiendishly hot sun, our tent not having yet arrived. Commander Limpus, of H.M.S. *Terrible*, assisted us in getting a good tent-raising-and-pegging scene. Shortly after we raised our own, and slept the sleep of the just.

December 9th —Our camp, though very pleasant in many respects, especially that of being associated with our courteous friends of the naval brigade, lacks one most important element, that of water. Two miles must we go for drinking water and a mile and a half for a wash, and for the horses to drink. Every drop in camp is guarded, and men cautioned not to be too free with their water-bottles. What would I not give for a good drink of water from some crystal

spring! We are drying up! Every night we are
obliged to get the password from the officers before
it gets dark, or woe be to us. I had fortunately
availed myself of the opportunity that evening,
while thanking Captain Jones for his kindness to
us, to ask for the password, which was "Aldershot,"
or I might have had to spend the night in some
other tent than my own ; for having strolled beyond

TENT RAISING AND PEGGING SCENE.

the limits of our camp to enjoy the delightfully cool
night breeze and a good Dutch cigar, I was suddenly
called to "Halt," at the point of a fixed bayonet, by
one of the sentries. On replying "Friend," I was
invited to approach and give the countersign. I
quickly spoke the word, and the answer came, "Pass,
friend." Of course I quite realised the importance
of this vigilance. Just as we were about to retire,
word came to me to be watchful and prepare to

decamp at any moment. What a night we spent creeping around, watching for a sign; our horses were harnessed in the dark and pegged up, and nearly all our packing done without a light, followed by a dismally quiet cup of coffee to keep the spirits up. But the move was not to be that night. The plan was to advance during the night, surprise the Boers at dawn with our big naval guns, and drive them from Chieveley or Colenso on up to the freeing of Ladysmith.

December 10*th*.—We visit the surrounding country to inspect the tremendous damage done by the Boers, and to scrutinise the positions they held a few days ago. On our return we enjoy a cold bath in the nearly dry stream, keeping a sharp look-out the while lest we be surprised by Boer looters. At last the word comes that we break camp at 2.30 a.m., and silently creep away before dawn. So after a pleasant hour's chat with our naval friends we pitch in and get everything ready for the 2.30 awakening. The sentinel who had received his orders from the Commandant to waken us at the appointed hour made his appearance, lantern in hand, at our tent door, announcing that we decamp at 3.30, December 11th. We were soon ready, tent down, pegs up and horses hitched, only awaiting the signal to advance, while drinking our coffee in the open. We, the highly favoured, followed in with the big guns drawn by bullocks and sailors, and I thanked my stars that I had broken rules, taken the bull by the horns, and was acting to suit myself.

About five we reached and passed the outposts, and naturally would have been sent back, but being in line with the guns and bullock waggons we passed on. Soon, however, we heard a loud voice, and Colonel Reeves rode up. " Hello, you there, Cape cart! How did you get there? You must fall out. Who are you?" I replied : " I am the representative of the Mutoscope and Biograph Company. Commander Limpus and Captain Jones know all about it." " Well, I must see about that," and

MILES OF BULLOCK WAGGONS.

off he rode with the escort, of which he had charge under General Barton.

The snap-shots show miles of bullock waggons and clouds of dust as we trek along in the rapidly increasing heat. We get to where the waggons are to stop for the night and unload, leaving our Zulu in charge, while we dash on to find the big iron tripod among hundreds of carts, it being impossible to carry it on our own Cape cart. The site having been selected, we get our guns in position ready to fire.

General Buller and General Barton are closeted, and the morning passes. The guns are inspected in the afternoon, then are placed in a splendid position facing Colenso, 9,000 yards distant. That night we only half pitched camp, and feasted on scraps of hard tack and tinned beef. Some good Samaritan brought us a large pot of soup and meat, which we had a hard time to get down. We slept almost out of doors that night, not having had time to put up our tent; besides, we did not think it worth while, as we had to move on at dawn a point nearer Colenso.

December 13*th*, at 7.10, we open fire on the enemy, our *Terrible* men doing marvellously good shooting, planting each shell just where it was needed, Boers flying right and left. On my way up to the guns early in the morning, as I was passing General Barton's tent he popped out, and seeing me stared for a moment, then said, " What are you? Where did you come from ? " I explained, and with a smile he replied, " Oh, that's it, is it ? " and passed on. Another danger averted. I have actually got to the point of dreading a recall or an idiotic set-back more than the enemy's shells. After the morning's bombardment, Captain Jones greeted me pleasantly and remarked, " Now are you happy? " " Yes," I replied, " the more I can get of the real thing the happier I shall be."

" Well, you'll get plenty more," he added. Strange how coolly we took the whole thing, considering the destruction it involved.

December 14*th*.—Not getting any reply from our neighbours, we decided to move on nearer, and leaving some guns behind, we took most of them with us to a hillock some 2,500 yards nearer to Colenso.

At early dawn we commence work again, and, as usual, stick to the guns, and being so far ahead we congratulate ourselves on our good luck in the two days' gunning, when no one was permitted to pass the

AFTER GETTING OUR PICTURES WE RETURN TO CHIEVELEY.

picket or outposts. After the shooting was all over and things comparatively safe, a stream of war correspondents could be seen making their way towards us from Frere Camp, that we had been forbidden to leave even after having General Buller's permission.

Never shall I forget the sensation of being within range of the Colenso guns while standing beside my

naval friends, who are firing shell and lyddite in rapid
succession into the fortification.   After getting our
pictures we left to return to Chieveley for food, six
miles from the front, our Cape cart and grey horses
offering a splendid mark for the enemy as we drove
along.   We soon discovered that nothing had come,
and starvation stared us in the face.   The stationmaster, however, took pity on us, and wired repeatedly to Frere for our grub to be sent on while
we waited.   Meanwhile we shared some black tea
with the soldiers, and finished our meal at the
stationmaster's dismantled and looted house, where
we found a good ham bone, bread, and jam.   What
a feast !   Being worn out mentally and physically I
lay down on a bed, covering my face with a meat
safe dish-cover to keep off the swarm of flies, and fell
asleep for five minutes.   My companion then coming
in, announced the arrival of our grub and other gear.
One half of this we soon packed, leaving the other
half at the station ; then pushed our way back again
to the guns.   We pass through camp after camp on
our way, practically all Frere Camp having moved up
that morning, commencing at daylight.   Miles and
miles of troops and transport waggons could be seen
wending their way across the twelve miles of field ;
indeed, as far as my eye could reach, every hill and
dale was covered with troops.   Just as we got back,
General Buller and some officers made their appearance on the hill.   As the General was walking away
from his horse he was snapped, standing and riding.
We could get only one Biograph of all this, though
magnificently effective, owing to the cloud of dust
caused by the recoil and concussion.   I was obliged
to ignore the kindly advice to stay on the opposite

GENERAL BULLER.

hill and take it from there by the telephoto ; but not being very sure of this new lens, I preferred to use my 8-inch Bausch and Lomb, and get within fifty feet instead of 1,500 yards or 2,500 yards. As soon, however, as we had taken the view, I had the machine dismantled and carried behind huge boulders for protection. Our horses, trembling and jumping at every shot, behaved splendidly, however, never moving from the spot, but scared out of their wits. My companions used cotton-wool in their ears to prevent the tremendous concussion, but as I wished to hear which way the shells were coming I preferred to drop the jaw at the word "Fire," a trick I learned at Sandy Hook, U.S., at the firing of the 10in., which answered the purpose very well.

It was a grand sight to watch the neat way our gunners dislodged the Boers, whom we could see running hither and thither, jumping on their horses and galloping off. Clouds of dust from many horse-men was all we wanted for guide as to where to shoot, and quickly our guns spoke in rapid succession with lyddite or ordinary shell, which must have demoralised them horribly. The shock caused by the terrific lyddite explosive will kill within a radius of a hundred feet by the mere concussion of air, and we could see the fortifications being blown sky-high in huge yellow columns of earth, stones, and men.

When all was over for the day, and our men had retired to rest, I went to the hill with Captain Jones and Commander Limpus to look at the Boer posi-tion through the large telescope. It was just getting dark, but it was still light enough to see the Boers creeping along round a hillock. The order was given, and quick as lightning our fine chaps jumped to their guns, raising clouds of dust as the shells exploded among the enemy.

We have made every effort to get a photograph of the Boer position, and the effect of the shots, by means of the telephoto, but we were forced to give it up owing to the haze and indistinctness which made it impossible to focus properly. There are many other difficulties besides, all of which I hope

CAPTAIN JONES AND COMMANDER LIMPUS VIEWING THE BOER POSITIONS.

to overcome in time. I shall then focus on the fortification and start our machine immediately after the shot has been fired, so as to see the effect. It is getting dark and our tent is not yet up, so we all pitch in, and are soon comfortably settled for the night, after rather a better supper than usual, having been fortunate enough to obtain some canned tomatoes to mix with our bully meat.

At 2.30, *December 15th*, we are, as usual, shaken

out. Oh, for some sleep ! We are nearly dead for
lack of rest and water ; the latter is so sadly wanted
that we cannot conscientiously use any for washing
purposes. We are miles from water, and we have
to keep our Zulu busy all day bringing supplies.
He generally returns, after one and a half hours'
walk, with some pitiable tale of thirsty soldiers and
an empty bucket. Even when the water reaches us

QUICK AS LIGHTNING OUR FINE FELLOWS JUMP TO THEIR GUNS.

we are besieged with applications which we are only
too happy to grant. Of course while our Zulu is
busy fetching and carrying, the brunt of the house-
work falls on us. For two days I haven't washed
my face, but if we survive the day and rush the
Boers from Colenso, nothing will keep us out of the
river, I am sure.

    To-day the great battle recommenced. At 4 a.m.
our guns opened fire, while our infantry slowly

advanced under cover of the naval guns, which kept up a steady action, bowling over the fortifications and shelters on the opposite side of the river.

But to return to to-day's battle, every detail of which I had the privilege of witnessing. While the guns were shelling, our men advanced across an open plain or valley, making straight for the river

AT 4 A.M. OUR NAVAL GUNS OPEN FIRE.

and Colenso bridge, in face of a deadly fire from the thousands of Boers who were well sheltered, while some of the wounded men were actually reduced to digging and tearing at the earth to hide their heads from the bullets. Our men were fired on for ten hours in the open, and were simply shot down and butchered. Some were ordered to cross the river, which had been dammed up by the Boers to make it twelve feet in depth and therefore impassable for our men. Some of the brave fellows nearly got drowned, notably the Dublin Fusiliers, who were weighted down with sixty pounds baggage and ammunition. The Boers had cleverly planned this, so that they could shoot the soldiers when once they were in the water and unable to defend themselves, and the ruse was carried out with considerable effect.

The bombs were bursting at our feet and tearing up the ground. All were ordered to "Get down under cover," which we did. Then a horrible thing happened. The Red Cross people were stationed close to our left, under command of my friend, Major Ricket, when the enemy commenced to shell this quarter deliberately, a shell bursting right among the Red Cross waggons, and inflicting great injury among the men and teams. It had been my original intention to join Major Ricket and the Red Cross staff, but I had been delayed trying to decide whether I would be able to secure a view of the guns. This hesitancy most likely saved the machine and Cape cart, and incidentally our skins. It is a marvel how anything escaped. When Commander Limpus commended me for choosing to stick to the guns instead of going with the Red Cross staff, he little knew how very close I was to going after all.

Soon we were all busy carrying in the wounded on stretchers, lifting them out of the Red Cross waggons and bearing them over huge boulders to the hospital, Colonel Reeves remarking to me as I passed, "This is hardly biographing." Some of the poor chaps whom we helped to take in were shot through head and stomach, and were most extraordinarily cheerful under the circumstances. I cannot dwell on the blood-curdling horrors I witnessed, the dying gasps and groans of agony. Brave lads! I was compelled to turn aside and busy myself in other matters. Meanwhile the bombardment was raging, many fortifications broken down and guns silenced. The most terrifying and

SOON WE ARE ALL BUSY LIFTING THE WOUNDED OUT OF THE RED CROSS WAGGONS.

demoralising sound I heard that day was the quick-firing Boer gun, which gave from four to five shots with only half a second between each. The roll of musketry was unceasing for hours, accompanied by the roar of our big twelve- and forty-pounders, none of which suffered at all. How heartily did we congratulate our naval officers on their good work and lucky escapes, five men only being wounded and one killed. At three o'clock it was understood both sides needed rest, and firing ceased. Not, however, until our men had rushed Colenso bridge, which proving too hot for them obliged us to retire for the day. We greatly fear our gallant artillerymen on our right have gone too far, as there is an awful scrimmage going on. It looks very much as if our guns would be taken.

That night we wandered out on the plain, supplied with the password, but it was too dark to see anything, so we decided to return, when in so doing we stumbled up against a Red Cross volunteer who was returning from burying some of his companions. When I suddenly called a halt it scared him nearly to death. We trudged back to camp through mealy patches and badly broken ground, stumbling at intervals with each other. He described the battle so graphically that I determined to visit the battlefield next day. Meanwhile we prepared our evening meal in our kraal, which we had hired for a change. We picked out a comparatively clean one and retired for the night. The Kaffirs fled for fear of the Boers and did not return for several days, and thus we had the unique experience of sleeping in a Kaffir kraal, on the soiled floor, with our heads near the door or hole entrance. We were so inexpressibly tired that the hard floor did not keep us awake, but slept soundly until 4 a.m., our usual hour of rising, varied occasionally by 2.30 a.m. For quite a while now we have had no full night's rest ; generally up or striking camp by star or moonlight, and trudging along in the dark.

Before retiring we felt impelled to visit the

hospital tents, where we witnessed some sights indeed. Among the dying we found our good and kind friend of the S.S. *Dunottar Castle,* Captain Hughes, who inoculated us all against the South African fever and thereby possibly saved our lives. He was shot while trying to help some sufferer on the field. How painfully near home this brings us.

SLEEPING IN A KAFFIR KRAAL (THE ONE IN BACKGROUND).

Saturday, 16th.—An armistice has been declared, and both sides profit by this to bury their dead. We search the river for a bath, and finding no pickets or outposts to object to our going, we stroll on towards the battlefield. Just as we got almost opposite to Colenso bridge we noticed three mounted Boers ; one seeing us made a dash for us, while we on our side prepared to give up the ghost or remain

A RED CROSS CORTÈGE WAS APPROACHING US.

prisoners. Stopping abruptly in front of us, I harangued him in German regarding the whereabouts of our dead. He said he would accompany us to the spot. *En route* he spied a wretched sheep; as quick as lightning he ran it down and with my penknife, which he borrowed, cut its throat and cleaned it. What he told us regarding his people was interesting, but we could gather no information from him that would be interesting to our side. I felt anxious to get rid of him, but he seemed determined to stay by us until we returned. Meanwhile we had picked up some Boer exploded shell, and strayed into the battlefield. I can only touch lightly on what I saw, and it was the most harrowing thing I ever witnessed. Khaki uniformed men lying about everywhere, deluged in blood, faces horribly distorted and swollen and black. A piece of shell had caught one in the head and opened up his brain. I was inexpressibly affected by the sight, and after covering up as many faces as we could, turned away. A Red Cross burying *cortège* was just then approaching us. The Boer, sitting his horse stolidly, counted within a few feet radius thirty-three dead, saying, " Poor fellows, poor fellows, what a pity ! " I asked him if he knew anything about the Biograph, and he said, Oh, yes, he had greatly enjoyed it at Johannesburg. I then inquired if he thought I could get some pictures from them later on ; at which he gave me a cordial invitation, saying he would speak to the General when I came.

I thought when the war was over, or nearly so, I might get something of interest from the other side without disloyalty to my people. His name he gave me as Commander Van Niekerk, and pointed to his home across the river.

We waited a little in order to see the burials, then trudged home through the most terrific sun I ever experienced. We had made so great a detour, that before we knew it we had walked from twelve to fifteen miles, whereas the real distance was not more than a mile. By the time we had reached a stagnant lot of water in the rapidly drying tributary near our camp, we were giddy with heat, and got into the deepest pool left, head over heels. I believe we just missed a sunstroke. We got into camp by quite another entrance, were challenged by the picket, then escorted into camp under arms. By and by, however, some one recognised us, and we were released.

I learned to-night that General Buller is greatly displeased that our men were led so far forward into the trenches. His plan was to show front only, and to draw most of the Boers away from Ladysmith. The wildest reports are abroad; General Buller is said to be shot in the leg, but by the time this reaches you, you will have proved the truth of this and other things. We are told that we must retreat to our first shelling position, and before 6 p.m. every camp had moved back to Chieveley with the exception of ourselves. I must confess to feeling somewhat uncomfortable for fear the Boers might attack us, and the remark of Commander Limpus did not tend to reassure me : " I hope they won't take a fancy to assault us, as our guns are not unlimbered."

At 2 a.m., December 17th, we crawled out of our Kaffir hut and finished packing by the rays of the moon, which, although full, was gradually disappearing under an eclipse. The weird half-light lasted until we had harnessed up our horses, then vanished, and we were obliged to set off in the deep gloom, our path only lighted by lanterns. Lanterns were about the worst thing we could have used, as it showed the enemy our movements. However, we drove along as quietly as possible and trusted to luck. We were especially anxious to avoid our guns being captured in the night. *En route* we had to pass through the burying and hospital grounds, and were

THE BURIALS.

almost overcome with the stench. At dawn we pitched camp, and after a six-o'clock breakfast we all collapsed. Sunday was a complete day of rest, no one daring to venture from their tents until after 5 p.m., the sun being unbearably hot.

December 18*th*.—Two miles in front of Chieveley camp, in view of Colenso, Tugela River in foreground. In order to be sure of the box getting through to the Castle Line people, I went to Durban accompanied by Seward, leaving Cox behind to guard the tent, &c. Cox drove us to the Chieveley station two miles off, where we waited three and a half hours for a freight car, changed at Estcourt at 10 p.m., rolled through the night, cold, supperless, and bedless, and arrived at Durban between 9 and 10 a.m. There we devoured a breakfast served *on a table !* nothing canned, and fresh bread and butter. What a treat ! After finishing all our work, shipping box, paying bills, getting fodder, &c., we took the night train back—not, however, before we had been pumped dry by every one we met regarding the Tugela repulse which we had just witnessed. It was a most difficult situation, for, much as I wanted to give free vent to my feelings, I felt debarred from doing so on account of my relations with the army.

On the train we were entertained by some red-hot angry Natal colonists who said we were making a mess of it all, and that if we would only back them up with men they would rush and bayonet the Boers and clear away the ground from Colenso to Ladysmith. The English, they said, sat around ; and when they did not do that they paraded, and when they did make a move they made it in the open, and so naturally lost their men. The Durban

people asked me repeatedly, " Do you think we shall
have to give it up ? Why doesn't General Buller let
us get a whack at them ? It is natural for us to
know the country better than the new arrivals. We
know every path and kloof."

Major McKenzie, in charge of the Carbineer
Volunteers, cried, it is said, when he was refused
permission to storm the enemy with his men. He
only asked for one thousand men, having laid all his
plans most carefully for the attack.

That night we again had to make the best of it—
no sleepers. Seward got off at Maritzburg to look
after any possible stray mail, &c. He didn't show
up for thirty-six hours, as the trains were irregular
and used only for carrying ammunition and food. I
got into Chieveley at 4 a.m., and tramped across the
veldt for two miles, till I reached our guns where
we have camped for weeks. As you may well know,
we are still keeping to the front so as to miss
nothing and always be able to see every move of
the enemy. This is a privilege which no other
civilian seems to have cared to attain. Occasionally
we are visited by correspondents and others when
our cannons roar. But to me the charm of it all is
in being on the spot where I can look down and
across to their lines and see a sudden dash of horse-
men from behind a clump of trees, making rapidly
for another, to be instantly fired into by our boys,
always with telling result, never failing to dislodge
the enemy from their covert. Our guns may truly
be said to be *the* life of this campaign ; and to the
guns I stick ! straying around whenever I wish, to
get a picture of anything interesting that may be
occurring. On returning we are always sure of a

kindly welcome from all our naval friends, from
Captain Jones, Commander Limpus (true types of
manly refinement and courtesy), down to the cook,
who supplies us with hot water whenever we feel
too worn out to heat any. All these things tend to
make our days more bearable. Our camp with the
guns is so far to the front that we hourly and
nightly expect to wake with a shell in our tent.
How we have escaped thus far is rather hard to tell.

We are doubtless almost surrounded by Boers,
whom our cavalry every now and then disperse in
admirable style. I am eagerly watching an opportunity to catch them as they dash out. Lord
Dundonald is kindness itself, and promises to let
me know, and if I can only be quick enough to seize
the right moment I shall have a superb picture.

December 19th.—After a smart piece of bombardment our naval friends succeeded in smashing the
Colenso bridge, thus preventing the enemy crossing
with their big guns and surprising us. It would
seem at first thought rather strange for us to do
this, as we expected shortly to cross ourselves; but
we had the information that they had undermined
the bridge with the intention to blow it up as we
crossed it, so we thought we'd do it for them, and
in three capital shots we did it. General Buller
highly complimented the skill of the gunner.

Strange signals are burning around us on all sides,
all along the mountains right and left of us. This
looks as though they were trying to attack us on all
three sides at once. Night shows their camp fires
far apart and reaching well to our rear. Should
their diabolical plan be to cut off our water supply,
we shall be in a blue way; the horses and cattle

now drink at a stagnant pool, and to-day that is reported nearly dry. All drinking-water comes from Frere by train every morning and evening. It is brought in ten huge five-hundred gallon tanks, and is distributed to the various camps in water tanks which are kept under strong military guard.

While at Frere I had pitched my camp at the very water's edge which was the drinking-water supply, and could judge of the quantity and the possibility of polluting it with dead horses and cattle, as is the Boers' wont, a thing very easily done although we have men patrolling the stream.

December 21st.—Scouts are out everywhere, riding hither and thither, quickly followed by small bodies of horsemen. Several of our men were out scouting, and, being very tired, dismounted and lay out on the grass, having placed one man on sentry duty. This poor fellow was surprised and shot by a party of Boers who came creeping up a dried river-bed before he could give the alarm. Our men, not having time to mount their horses, took to their heels, two of them scrambling on one horse. I was watching it all through glasses, when I noticed the two men on the one horse stop, leaving one man to make his way up to us while the other rode back furiously to try and help his comrades who, while running, had been pelted with bullets. One other man was killed besides the sentry. On the horseman's return to his comrades he found the other horses all shot and the men still making towards camp. Meanwhile Major McKenzie had been informed of the circumstance, and with one hundred horse urged by voice and spur to the utmost speed dashed out to the rescue, the Major calling out lustily the while,

" Up, Carbineers ; our boys are in danger ! " And
so this kind of thing goes on day after day, the most
exciting scenes keeping us for ever on the *qui vive*.

December 22nd.—The guns are booming as we are
at breakfast. We are getting quite fond of the
sound, and we delight in watching the destruction
of the enemy's well-built entrenchments as they

RECONNOITERING IN FORCE.

disappear in a cloud by a skilfully directed shell.
As fast as they build we endeavour to destroy.

Saturday, December 23rd.—Through Lord Dundonald's kindness I am informed of a sortie, and we
get away, cutting across country. Meeting the
party, who point to the kopje, we turn our cart containing the machine on to the spot, they meanwhile,

very kindly keeping away from the machine. In spite of the rush I feel sure we must have a good and most valuable picture. They ride up sharply, dismount, lead the horses back, and the men advance to the edge of the kopje to hide among the rocks. This was the first kopje. Not finding the enemy, they mount again and gallop to the next, and so on until they do find the enemy, whom they quickly drive off. I need not add that this was a *tour de force*, carried out in spite of the fact that our horses were only half hitched up, and that we had to drive at a gallop across country to intercept the horsemen.

After we had secured this valuable picture I thought it unadvisable to follow on to the next kopje, as we doubtless would be fired on sooner or later. We ran some risk, of course, but the danger was slight compared to the next kopjes; this of course we didn't know, and we enjoyed the excitement of the enterprise. On our return we were much amused to meet Colonel Sitwell riding solemnly along with a Christmas chicken fastened to his saddle. It caused us all much merriment.

Just then it occurred to me that a panoramic or bird's-eye view of the artillery, cavalry, naval and Irish Fusilier camps, that are so far in advance of the other camps, would prove interesting, and furthermore would give the public an idea of the surrounding country. The view starts with Lord Dundonald's cavalry, transport waggons, tents, camps and artillery, and the remnant that is left of the various Irish Fusilier regiments, including our naval camp on the central hill nearest the enemy, with the Colenso hills beyond. This shows about one tenth of the camps, which reach away back to Frere, and are so scattered that I thought it well to secure these camps before they moved. For you know it is only one bugle call, then ten minutes later another, and every tent comes down and the trekking commences.

December 24*th*, *Christmas Eve.*—There are no signs of the enemy; our cannons are resting. I think it must be mutually agreed on to keep the peace for a day or two. While out driving around in search of subjects for the Biograph, and grub for man and beast, I called on Lord Dundonald, and was again helped in getting a good picture. Some picket was to be reinforced, and we got a company of the 13th Hussars *en route* to the picket, Lord Dundonald telling them to gallop as they passed the Biograph on their way. This they did with fine effect. It is a wonder to me that any one can brave the fierce rays of the sun to play football, and yet it may be seen going on in every camp during a respite.

I am getting rather more accustomed to the heat, although I cannot say it is enjoyable, and I hardly think I would dare attempt, much as I would like, to join in a football game. If it would only rain! A heavy thunderstorm is now threatening to break on us, but we fear it will pass us by. It is at present, however, a grand sight. Two heavy black clouds have risen from almost opposite points of the compass, to meet overhead in flame and thunder. At first we noticed a cloud rise in the west, divide, and then circle around to north and south, and finally directly up over us. For a while we had a little excitement driving down pegs and getting ready: our enemies, however, got it when the storm really burst. We did hope for rain to replenish our dried-up streams, for even if we did not get it at this precise spot, its coming in the vicinity will benefit us indirectly. (The subject of the illustration below has just stopped my pen.)

South Africa may have much to recommend it, but for me as I feel at this present moment I would rather endure dear old London's worst winter fog and mud indefinitely than go through an experience I had ten minutes ago. Directly above my head this huge tarantula made his appearance, and received a crushing blow with this book. In an instant all of us, in response to my yell, were turning up every piece of furniture, chips, sod, and what not, each man with a candle in hand. The spider was only wounded when I found him under my satchel, and I held him down while one of my companions got a bottle in which we secured him for the unbelieving. This has started my collection, and to-day, Christmas, after a crawly and uncomfortable night, we add two scorpions to our collection. Almost every loose stone harbours these reptiles.

As soon as the camps hear of our adventures and subsequent collection, we were overwhelmed with such courtesies as the following, " We heard you was collectin' them things," and a Tommy Atkins appears at our tent door with one of these specimens held between two sticks.

While vainly attempting to prevent some horrible insect from drowning in my coffee, I question my visitor as to the possibility of getting several scorpions and tarantulas for a fight before the Biograph.

Biographing in South Africa —
unwelcome visitors to our tent

Tarantula
actual size

Head of a
Tarantula
showing sting in centre.

Trap-door Spider
medium size

Common Centipede —
found under the biscuit box

Specimen of a
fair sized Scorpion
found under my cot —

Trap door Spider
and nest.
dug out at
Chieveley Camp
near Colenso.
Jan 7th
1900

To the
Unbelievers in S. African pests, this page is
most humbly dedicated —
The above actual sized Tarantula and
Scorpion, were Biographed in one round,
and their remains I carefully embalmed
and sent to England — Jan. 25th 1900

W.K.L. Dickson

Upper Valley of the Tugela
near Ladysmith, Natal

(The sketch is reduced to less than half in size.)

We hitch up and drive around among the camps to witness the distribution of plum-puddings, &c., the chocolate not having yet arrived.

In the afternoon I suggested my pet picture to some members of our Naval Brigade, who immediately jumped at the idea and worked hard to carry it out. I proposed a tug-of-war with John Bull and Kruger *en costume.* They were to fight, John Bull, of course, is to sit down on Kruger. The taking of these scenes, together with the subsequent events of the day, illustrated the absolute indifference to danger which characterised the troops. Although in full sight of the enemy we had a jolly good day, dining with the Naval Brigade and taking part in the performance of the evening, composed of stories, refreshments and songs. Commander Limpus and his officers looked in upon us for a while, and Captain Jones and some others accepted the invitation to supper. The wording of the invitation caused some amusement; it ran thus : " Come to supper, and bring your own knife and spoon." When these officers departed we escorted them down the hill to the clatter of knife and fork.

In regard to the Christmas pictures, I will add that I arranged the details of the tug-of-war with the assistance of Gunner Baldwin, chief instructor, and others. First, Kruger and John Bull pull against each other ; then we have the former hanged and buried in great state, a bodyguard presenting arms and a minister in attendance. Another picture of John Bull laying down the law. It is needless to say that the proceedings of Christmas Day comprised toasts to our wives and sweethearts.

It is delightful to see how well the naval volunteers

and the Naval Brigade fraternise. Yesterday, in com-
pliment to their friends of the *Terrible* and *Forte* the
volunteers sent them a large supply of fruit, beer
and other refreshments, which were greatly needed
and much appreciated.

I have just met Colonel Hamilton, who stopped
me with the inquiry, " Where did you come from ? "
I told him. After several other questions he said
that I had been reported to him as missing, and that
he was very glad to see me. I had not been seen
after the battle. My Cape cart had been reported
injured.

I expect we shall be captured or shelled before we
get through. We are always skirmishing around
and escaping in our Cape cart, in search of photographs during the day, and at night we camp with
the Naval Brigade, the position of which suits better
than that of the other camps, inasmuch as it is
always considerably in advance. We get quite
fascinated with this mode of living, and would soon
find the orthodox ways of the bigger camps tame in
comparison.

There is much discussion among the officers
regarding this war crisis, especially in connection
with our last repulse ; we are even talking about
going back to Frere Camp. We'll see. Of course
the water supply there would be an inducement.
There is also talk of flanking the enemy, going
around, as the Colenso hills seem impregnable.

December 26*th.*—Camp near Colenso (Chieveley).
A furious dust storm has arisen, and it is all we
can do to hold down our tent and breathe. We
are suffocated, and can only fill our lungs with air
by breathing through a handkerchief while struggling

with the ropes and inflated tent. We get the brunt
of the storm, being poised on the very top of the
hill—a meeting place for all the breezes of heaven.
After a while the wind and sand storm changed to a
heavy downpour, varied with lightning, and it was
not long before we were flooded out of our tent, the

A RECONNOITRE IN FORCE.

water rushing in and passing under our cots, upon
which we had piled everything of value. It is not
easy to give an idea of the horrors and discomfort of
a wet tent. There was nothing to choose between
the outside and the inside. However, as rain is
much needed, we must try to endure these incon-
veniences.

8

December 27*th.*—We rose at 6 a.m., rather stiff, but otherwise none the worse for the wetting. The usual weekly box of films, snap-shots, and MSS. was prepared for London, and Seward carried it to Maritzburg.

Later in the day another storm came on, and many of our sailor lads and Tommies got a good bath by stripping and running about in the rain, some bathing in the recesses of the huge tarpaulins covering the ammunition waggons.

December 28*th.*—Another awfully wet night. We are all rheumatic and cold, and it is impossible to get dry. Our oil lamp even won't keep lighted. For hours we toiled with spade and shovel, digging deeper trenches and using other expedients to keep out the rain and storm, but all to little effect. Cox is sick and Seward little better, but I am wonderfully well. Seward made his appearance at breakfast, with the news that the London box had been dispatched, and brings new supplies. Our men are digging trenches all round the hill to protect the camp and guns from a sudden attack, operations which oblige a little settlement or kraal directly below the guns and entrenchments to remove themselves further down the hill.

There is much talk and considerable excitement among the natives, who do not relish this enforced flitting. However, they finally choose it in preference to being in the direct line of the shooting. I was much interested in watching the methods by which the kraals are moved. First the thatching or long grassy straw is taken from the roof and sides, and the sooty frame or basket bared. Then twenty or more blacks, with song and gesture, carry

this huge basket on their shoulders to the new settlement. One man in a strong, high-pitched voice screams
a few inarticulate words, which are instantly taken
up as a chorus in a deeper key, keeping perfect
time. The leader gets more and more excited as
the chant proceeds, springs from the ground and
beats the soil at intervals with his knobbed stick.
Gradually the infectious enthusiasm spreads to the
carriers and the chorus swells into a roar of approval.
They present a most uncanny sight these savages,
toiling away with perspiration pouring down their
huge naked black bodies, which are ornamented with
beads and ear pegs. The women do little more than
gather the household goods and blackened straw for
the next camping ground, and are rarely seen with
the men, usually preferring to sit apart in a circle,
arranging their hair or wool by the aid of a piece of
broken mirror. I might add that from the snap-shots
sent it will be seen that these women seem to con-
sider garments as a superfluous luxury ; a few beads
often comprising the entire costume. It is wonderful, however, how well these look on their rich brown
velvety skin. I tried to purchase one of these beaded
arrangements, but had regretfully to give it up, as I
understood from the lady in question that it formed
her entire wardrobe. I think they have taken my
order for one, but am not sure, it being a difficult
and delicate matter to make my meaning clear. I
had no knowledge of their dialect, so had to resort to
gesture, nature's universal language.

On my return to my tent I found another batch of
tarantulas, scorpions, and other abominations awaiting me. I had made known the fact that I wanted
a few of these specimens to biograph them fighting,

if possible, and now the boys keep bringing endless numbers of these horrible creatures, which we stow away in separate compartments, having learned from experience that the stronger devour the weaker ; a truly appalling sight. Our present list of captured reads : four huge tarantulas, fourteen scorpions, three centipedes, two snakes (black, flat-headed and poisonous), no end of curious bugs, insects and worms ; three chameleons, a pet kitten, a puppy dog, and a huge trap-door spider.

Friday, December 29*th.*—We are all so damp in our tent that we have had to carry everything out of doors and roll the tent back to profit by a few hours of sunshine. In doing so we killed several scorpions and other loathsome reptiles which have been comfortably ensconced under our beds. We had plenty of time for these operations, as little or nothing is happening in connection with the enemy, unless it be an occasional small skirmish with the Boers who venture too near us.

Desiring to see a little more of Boer doings I rode out to the lines, keeping at a safe distance from their rifles, and was rewarded by a good view of their fortifications, together with an excellent description of their methods and plans from a bright scout who accompanied me to each successive kopje.

Our companions are a little better, which is a great relief to my mind, as so many men have had to give in during the last few weeks and go to the hospital.

The evening was spent with some friendly officers, who visited our tent in order to post us as to a move of some kind soon to take place.

Saturday, December 30*th.*—Fine weather at last,

so we again commence our preparations to photograph a tarantula and scorpion set-to. It is a unique if unpleasant subject. A tin box was made with glass front, and after several bloodthirsty and blood-curdling rehearsals, in the course of which they actually devoured each other, they were taken. The rehearsals had to be abbreviated on account of these cannibalish tendencies. Once when we had left a batch together overnight, we found it in the morning greatly increased in rotundity while decreased in numbers.

The fight took place amid cheers from a host of soldiers and sailor lads. The combatants had to be poked up at first, but they warmed to their work most satisfactorily. We have had such a sickening of the whole thing, that the subject is now a forbidden one in our camp; yet these specimens still continue to flow in, and we cannot arrest the tide. A very large flat-headed, poisonous snake appeared in our tent this morning. It had crawled out of a tin box at our tent door, through the curiosity of an officer who was anxious to see the reptile, and then could not get the cover on again. So we have another boarder, for he eluded our first search and obliged us to spend the night with him, as we were too busy all day long to engage in a reptile hunt.

There was talk of attacking the Boers to-night, and had the night been clear and not so bitterly cold and wet the affair might have come off. It was arranged that a few of our troops should advance under cover of night in the neighbourhood of their new trenches, and fire rapidly, under the supposition that this would draw the Boers down into the trenches. Then at a given moment our large naval guns would fire a volley (and as our gunners have proved themselves crack shots they would effect deadly work in the trenches). The guns during the day had been carefully trained on these trenches, and after the recoil of the guns each had been replaced and resighted from three fixed points in line with the trenches ; a most clever plan.

After two hours' waiting in dead silence and bitter cold, through a soaking rain we decided to retire for the night, as evidently our mounted cavalry never went out : for we did not hear their fusilade, and so we did not fire to support them.

Sunday, December 31st.—We are again without food for our horses, and there is none to be had for love or money. Grazing is nil, and as we have had two days of this now, we'll have soon to go on a foraging expedition to see what we can find. Hunting for pictures is not all that is to be done here, as may be seen from this circumstance. While out we were much interested to see how the soldiers were building up stone walls and digging trenches to fortify our stronghold against sudden attack ; for should there be an attempt to get our guns, there would undoubtedly be a frightful battle for supremacy. The Boers recognise equally with ourselves the indispensability of these weapons.

We find forage for the horses and some bread, so that as far as food is concerned we can keep alive for another day. We hurry back just in time to watch our neighbours' newly built fortifications crumble beneath the unerring marksmanship of our bluejackets.

January 1, 1900.   Chieveley Camp, near Colenso. —Great firing this morning for several hours, which

ROYAL FUSILIERS STRIKING CAMP.

attracted a lot of correspondents from Frere Camp,
six and a half miles away.   The shooting had ceased
when they arrived, and so they returned to camp,
which seems very hard, as it is certainly most difficult for them to be on hand at the exact moment.
The firing doubtless was to cover our brave chaps of
the 13th Hussars and B.M.I.'s.   At the same time
Thornycroft's Mounted Infantry made a daring dash
for the Umhlangeni Hill on the right flank, and got
sufficiently near to draw the enemy's fire from the
trenches used at the Colenso fight.   After an hour's
fusilade our men took cover from the Maxim-
Nordenfelt's deadly one-pound shots, which still
issue from a concealed spot.   Our men got off
scathless ; some Boers are reported killed.   Our
extreme forward position enables us to witness these
occurrences by the aid of a good spyglass, but unfortunately they are not within biographic distance.

January 2nd.—The usual 4 to 6 a.m. early breakfast is despatched to our Boer neighbours in the
shape of lyddite shells, a performance which we
have learned to sleep through tranquilly.   At least
we hear them, for of course each shot nearly shakes
us out of our cots, but we are asleep again before the
next one is fired.   I never could have believed this
possible had I not tested it personally.

Lord Dundonald passed our tent this morning
while we were at breakfast, to tell me that there was
to be a sortie against the enemy, if I cared to take
the troops riding out.   Before going we catch an
excellent picture of our Royal Fusiliers striking
camp, while those who are ready march past.
Lord Dundonald was at the head of the South
African Light Horse Infantry, accompanied by

Major McKenzie, Major Graham, and Captain Birdwood, followed later by Captain Denney and Captain Campbell.   Of course, as a rehearsal was impossible I could only ask them to round and come towards me, which they did with fine effect.

The object of the sortie was to repel the Boers, who were encroaching on our territory and seriously

LOCOMOTIVE AND CARS BEING ARMOURED IN A NEW WAY.

hampering us by trying to invade our water supply. On our return to camp we took a most interesting picture of a locomotive and cars being armoured in a new way.   Our bluejackets, under the direction of Chief Gunner Instructor Baldwin, have matted together tons of heavy rope and covered doubly the whole engine, making it, we believe, bomb proof.

The picture shows the men hoisting up the rope

mats, while others are making them ; soldiers on the tender cheering.

A yell from my companions announces the fact that a big snake has been found coiled up comfortably under the provision box. Our neighbours crowd in to see the killing of a very poisonous reptile, our room-mate for the last three days.

Everybody is greatly excited over the coming of Lord Roberts and Lord Kitchener, and if they come to Durban first instead of Capetown, we will try to get the landing. I do not expect them this way though.

Time for the box to go, so must stop.

Thursday, January 4, 1900. Chieveley Camp, near Colenso.—We are still here and our people are extremely restive and crazy to get at the enemy. No orders have yet come, however. We see the officers at all times of the day studying the enemy's position and holding council as to how best to attack it. Among the more conspicuous of the officers are General Buller, General Clery, General Barton, and our friends Captain Jones and Commander Limpus.

No guns fired to-day.

Friday, January 5th.—My companions are up and about, having recovered from their indisposition, while I have to take my turn, not being able to leave my tent. Our neighbours are most solicitous and kind, and entertain us with their experiences in travel, spinning the most extraordinary yarns for our amusement. Among other things the South African Admiralty came under discussion, and in not too complimentary terms. It is stated (with what accuracy I cannot say) that they put every imaginable obstacle in the way of our Naval Brigade's getting their guns immediately to the front, and that it was only by strategy that the feat was accomplished.

January 6th.—Water is getting worse and worse and the heat intense.   Both Captain Jones and Commander Limpus have collapsed, so I am in illustrious company.   This is bad, considering what a severe day's work we have before us.

Ladysmith was attacked at early dawn by the Boers, who were repelled three times with great losses on both sides.   Hour after hour we listened to the bombardment, which must have been terribly destructive, for there was hardly a minute's let-up on either side.   The whole atmosphere is indescribably shaken and torn.   Now is our turn to act, or Ladysmith may be overwhelmed.   We must draw the Boers towards us and away from Ladysmith by storming them.

Sharp at 2.30 the cavalry, artillery, and troops again rapidly cross the open, hoping to draw the enemy's fire and to make the Boers believe that we intended to rush across and storm Colenso, but in spite of a brisk cannonading from our artillery which had approached very close to the Boer lines, we receive no encouragement to continue very long. Our position was well in advance of a small kopje which we had once occupied, and from which we had been obliged to retire after the battle of Colenso.

As soon as we saw the troops filing out, followed by Lord Dundonald's cavalry and artillery, we lost no time in harnessing up our horses and dashing down the hillside to the accompaniment of our

naval guns, which are fully employed covering the
British advance. So far as we can tell, the plan
was a success. The Boers evidently thought they
were being stormed at Colenso, and left the Lady-
smithians alone for a while. In the meantime
dense black clouds were forming in the sky and
gave us fair warning of the approach of a severe
storm, which broke furiously upon us about 5 p.m.

The Boers made no reply to the English attack
except to fire shrapnel from their upper guns on the
hills, the shells bursting in mid-air with terrific
detonations but fortunately causing us no damage.

On our return to camp we found that some of
the soldiers of the Union Brigade who had halted
near our tent had somehow got in and looted everything edible, much to our indignation and that of
our naval friends, who made every effort to discover the thieves and secure compensation for our
losses. This was very serious indeed, as we were in
hourly expectation of a trek and could not take
time to replenish our stores from Durban. This
disaster necessitated considerable foraging from
canteens and friendly neighbours, who never
failed to respond, there being a marked feeling of
good comradeship towards us and a cordial appre-
ciation of our endeavour to record their doings by
means of the Biograph and notes.

January 8th.—Much to our joy, we received word
this morning to hold ourselves in readiness for a
trek. The news is welcome, as we are heartily sick
of this long and apparently useless wait. The
camps are all alive cleaning up and repairing things,
and there is a healthy bustle everywhere. From
early dawn every available soldier has been at work

digging fortifications around our gun-hills, such as deep trenches and earth-works, with here and there stone entrenchments. While I am scribbling this in bed, Captain Jones feebly strolls over to my tent for a chat. He is not much better that I can see, and on inquiry I find that Commander Limpus is very feverish and prostrated. The news of our early departure has, however, acted like a charm, and I myself feel already better in the very thought of a change. During the night we were aroused by an alarm—" Enemy approaching! To arms!" At 11.30 p.m. the men were awakened, ordered to fix bayonets, to remain still, not to show a light, and to await orders. Hours passed in breathless anticipation of an attack, but our outposts had been at fault, they had mistaken a large herd of cattle for the enemy—not very complimentary to the followers of Oom Paul.

January 9th.—Our horses are down with a bad case of influenza, brought on doubtless by repeated wettings, as we have no shelter at night for them. We have therefore had to look around for some pieces of tarpaulin as a protection against the pouring rain, their blankets being quite inadequate. We ourselves make the best of the situation under canvas, and devote ourselves to getting ready for a sudden call.

Crash! Out we rush *en déshabille*, to find our two-wheeled vehicle fallen backwards and our horses rearing and plunging around the *débris*. After politely assuring the horses that the accident was due to the excessive weight of the Biograph, and not their fault, we brought the cart back into position and put the iron tripod on the shaft to keep it down. As usual, the camera, or Biograph, remained uninjured. It seems to have a charmed life.

Towards evening we rode around to visit our friend Captain Wild, in whose charge are several of the naval twelve-pounders. He was encamped on an exquisite spot, a high bluff overlooking Chieveley Camp on one side and the blue distant mountains of Zululand on the other. I gazed on the latter with indescribable longing to explore, the more so as I had received a cordial invitation from one of the chiefs to visit his kraal, which he described as set in a beautiful, sunny land, rich with trees, meadows, and rivers, and surrounded by towering mountains.

On the other side of one of those peaks was enacted the great murder of an entire tribe by King Chaka. The king of the Zulus held sway over a distant tribe who had not paid him tribute for some years. He ordered them all, men, women, and children, to trek to his kraal to do him homage and to bring him gifts. Meanwhile Chaka had taken a position on a high hill above a deep chasm or cañon, over the brink of which he drove them, they singing his praises the while. The chasm is said to be several hundred feet deep, and was filled with the dead and dying. Every Zulu knows the story.

I could not devote much time to contemplation, however, for it was necessary to partake of our host's good cheer and to inspect the new fortifications and gun-pits together with the other merits of this well-chosen spot of defence.

The Commander sends word that we trek to-

morrow at 4.30 a.m.   Good!   Later on we receive
a visit from Captain Jones, who informs us that the
hour has been postponed to 8.30.   With his usual
kindly consideration he had come round to let us
know, so that we could get a good sleep.

Wednesday, January 10th.—Breakfast over, we
pack away our best belongings, strike camp, and
by 8.30 are trekking with the rest.   The utmost
secrecy has been observed in regard to the dummy
4.7 guns left on the hill in place of the real ones
which accompany us, and which have been taken
apart and packed under our tents so as not to be
visible to the enemy in the event of their examining
us through glasses.   It was part of our usual good
fortune that all this was done next to our tent.
The building of the dummies took place right under
our eyes, whereas sentries were placed in every
direction to keep all the other civilians at bay.   The
intention is to keep firing as usual, morning and
evening, with the two twelve-pounders placed near
the dummies.   Meanwhile, if the army succeeds in
getting round to the west of Ladysmith, a trek of
from thirty-three to thirty-five miles, and can plant
our 4.7 guns without being discovered, we shall
have gained a point, and a good one.   All we fear
is some skulking spy.

So we leave " Liar's Hill," which I quite believe
has deserved its title, for, as Captain Jones says, he
has heard more wonderful stories there of things
which were about to be done and which never came
about than he could possibly enumerate.   Trekking
is no easy business, and if it were not for the
courtesy of the Naval Brigade's commanders we
could not carry all our effects.   This is one of the

many good reasons which induce us to stick to the
guns.   Moving in line with hundreds of waggons,
ten or twelve miles in length (not the waggons, but
the space covered), is slow work, and so we stop off,
first at one camp and then another, to say goodbye
to those who remain behind.   Presently we were
spied by a red-headed Scotchman, and invited to
have breakfast with him.   He was compounding
some kind of bread out of flour, baking-powder, and
water in a greasy pan over a wood fire ; and after
partaking of this, together with some oatmeal, bacon,
and coffee, we moved on.   This is the way we live,
from hand to mouth, never knowing where we shall
get the next meal.   Oh for Pretoria under the
British flag !

We fall into line again, occasionally getting ahead
of the waggons when the road is wide, and bending
our efforts to catching up with the Naval Brigade.

Towards 2 p.m. and at a certain angle we meet
the whole of Frere Camp going in the same direction, the cavalcade having the appearance of a huge
reversed **Y**.

Towards 6 p.m. we approach an awful ford, in
which every transport waggon sticks and has to be
hauled out by double and treble ox-teams, and so
the work goes on so slowly that we dread being left
on the road without shelter for the night.   I therefore pushed on to the edge of the river and waited
my chance, carefully noting the one and only narrow
possible crossing.   We waited until one waggon had
got over successfully by the help of thirty - six
bullocks, and then made the attempt.   The other
side was crowded with our friends, who were
encouraging the rest of us to hurry, the night being

nigh at hand ; so under the impetus of whip and voice my thoroughbreds tumbled me and the cart safely across and up the steep embankment, encouraged by the cheers of our friends. My two companions waded after. Our steeds were highly complimented on their sturdy pull and on not getting out of the narrow, rocky bottom, which, if they had done, would have resulted in an upset. As soon as the disguised big guns and baggage had

ONE WAGGON, DRAWN BY THIRTY-SIX BULLOCKS, CROSSING THE DRIFT.

crossed we fell into line, but were soon to have another set-back. An officer rode up and laughingly informed us that there was another and far worse crossing before us which would have to be made at night. Cheerful intelligence !

At dusk we reached the big ford, and there we stuck. It was almost impossible for any of the transports to cross. Mile after mile, stretching halfway back to Frere and Chieveley, the roads were black with waggons and men. Our Naval

9

Brigade had succeeded in edging their waggons up
to the ford, so as to wait their turn to cross. I left
the Cape cart to find some way over the river, and
heard an officer say, " I wish somebody would risk
that bridge." " Where ? " I asked, and was shown
in the gathering gloom a structure apparently hardly
capable of bearing more than one cart. On my way
I met Chief Gunner Instructor Baldwin, who went
with me to inspect, after which I agreed to pioneer

STEAM TRANSPORT CROSSING PRETORIUS DRIFT.

the bridge, provided the sailors would pull me out
if I got stuck. Returning to where I had left the
cart, all of us made for the wooden structure, each
of my assistants guiding a horse over ploughed fields
and mealy patches to the crossing. Giving the
horses a good breathing spell, I guided them slowly
and with extreme care, keeping to the centre of the
narrow bridge, they snorting and slipping, falling
through some of the planks, which so frightened

them that they tore up the almost perpendicular sides of the embankment. This embankment had been dug down considerably by the able corps of Royal Engineers, but the recent work had rendered the soil so extremely soft that we again stuck. After ten minutes' time Instructor Baldwin returned with his willing sailor lads, and to the tune of " All together, boys," we reached the top, only to discover that it was now night and about to rain ; also that we were alone and cut off from our people, besides being on the high road, the order having been countermanded for the advance. All were to halt where they were till dawn. Meanwhile we were tentless, the Cape cart filled to overflowing and affording very little protection beneath it from wind and rain, so we simply decided to sit up all night.

Just as the rain commenced we spied, between lightning flashes, a transport waggon covered with tarpaulin. To this we drove, and hid ourselves among highly odoriferous naked Kaffirs. We stood them as long as possible, and then fled. The rain ceased after a while, and was succeeded by a brilliant moon, illuminating the whole surrounding country, and more particularly a tumbled down mud-built house, for which we made immediate tracks. Leaving the cart on the road carefully fastened up, we carried our bedding across a deep ditch to the house, 50 to 75 feet distant, and there settled down in the porch (January 11th). Soon the clouds came up again and all was pitch dark. I was lying awake, too tired to sleep, while my companions were snoring, when suddenly I thought I heard some one at the cart. In an instant I had

run across the plot of ground and floundered through
the ditch, with mud halfway up my boots, just in
time to discover a lot of troopers looting the cart
of its contents. As soon as I yelled they retreated
in the gloom, carrying with them everything we had
in the shape of food, cups, dishes, cooking utensils,
and all our film and plates. I tried to catch sight of
the regiment's letters, or to get a helmet off their
heads, but in vain. They had left chaos behind
them. Everything had been thrown out on the
muddy ground : our water bag and bottles, lime-
juice, &c., &c., gone ! The situation could not
have been worse, and after the first wave of anger
and fight had past, I found myself laughing im-
moderately at the ruin they had left behind. This
simply meant that we had to return to Durban
via Frere, thence by rail to Durban, and back—a
distance estimated at 625 miles. On our return
we should have to catch up with our naval people,
who most probably might have had to fight in the
meantime, and we not there to record the event.
It was heart-rending, more especially as I had no
sleep for three nights, having been in a constant
state of suspense.

Our sad plight reminded me of the American
pioneer ranchman, who, after a year's absence,
returned to find only a few smoking embers in
place of what had once been a prosperous farm,
peopled by wife and children, servants and cattle,
and stored with all the accumulated comforts won
by ten years' hard toil. No words came to him but,
" Well, this is too ridiculous for anything." I
remembered the story, and, applying it, laughed.

It was now 1 a.m., and I spent the rest of the

night moon-gazing and awaiting the dawn, when I awoke my companions to assist in unpacking the Biograph, &c., from the cart. Fortunately for us the camera had not struck the looters' fancy. We carried the Biograph and appendages into the house, and, leaving Cox in charge, Seward and I went back on horseback across the ford. Still breakfastless and cold, we rode to the quarters of our friends of the Naval Brigade, who were sitting around the waggons drinking coffee and feasting on adamant biscuits and bully beef. A chorus of indignation and disgust greeted the repetition of our story. I then carried a cup of coffee and some eatables back to the house, telling Cox he must forage and do the best he could for himself, after which I joined Seward and commenced our long trek back, first stopping to get a view of the bridge which we had crossed the night before, and which had been partially washed away by the night's flood. This fact made me very thankful that I had not postponed the crossing.

We reached Frere after many hours of hard riding, only to find that there was no train until 9 p.m. After getting our horses stabled and paying an extravagant price for some supper we took train for Maritzburg, arriving there at 4 a.m., January 12th. We attended to some business, then continued our journey by the 9 a.m. train, reaching Durban at 1.30 p.m. Every one we met begged for news, which we gave with the utmost caution. We were the only people direct from the front—a fact which was sufficiently evident from our appearance, our khaki dress, and the mud with which we were covered. After getting food, film, &c., we

returned by the 5.40 p.m., and at two the next
morning (January 13th) we were wakened from a
sound sleep at Mooi River by the night sentries
swinging a lantern in our eyes. After examining
General Buller's pass they allowed us to go on to
Frere, which we reached at 5 a.m., sore and hungry.
There we had a hard time trying to persuade the
proprietors of a little temporary inn to get up and
give us some coffee. After a good deal of talk, and
a considerable outlay of time and coin, we left Frere
on our two half-starved beasts, which, despite their
weakened condition, had to carry over fifty pounds
each of food, film, blankets, and overcoats, in
addition to the riders. When we reached the spot
where we had left Cox and the cart we were so
exhausted that for two hours we lay upon our
blankets unable to say a word. Suddenly we sensed
the delicious odour of a chicken stew, which
effectually aroused us. Cox was the cook, and his
stew was delicious. After dinner we found ourselves
able to discuss our plans with a good deal more
interest. Good food is inspiring, and especially so
after a long course of hard tack, bully beef, and other
horrible canned stuffs. To be suddenly introduced
to a savoury dish of this kind was almost more than
our nerves could stand.

The chicken was soon a thing of memory, but
even then powerfully reminiscent. We knew it
would be good to talk about when the mouldy bread
and hard tack and muddy water again fell to our
portion. We could enter into the feelings of the
unlucky Southern soldiers who were playing audience
to a thrilling recital of how a huge waggon-load of
hams had been rationed out to their Northern ene-

mies; of how dozens of succulent slices could be
seen spluttering in the frying-pans, making the air
thick with appetising odours. Fancy this story in
the ears of men who had been living for months and
months on plain corn meal and other insipid cereals.
One poor soldier could stand it no longer, and burst
out with, "Pard, oh pard, say them greasy words
again."

I forgot to mention in its proper sequence an incident in connection with the collapse which preceded
our banquet. I was lying prone, too tired to move
or breathe, when a hen walked in and meandered all
around me and twice up my muddy leg, as if select-
ing a spot suitable for business. She settled down
at last near my right shoulder. I offered no inter-
ference at the time, but when she had retired I
reached out dispassionately and despatched the
contents of the egg. I felt like an up-to-date
edition of Elijah and the ravens.

By three in the afternoon our belongings were
packed, and we were ready to move on, so as to
catch up, if possible, with our party. We took
turns at the reins, two of us walking. For hours
we trudged along until at about 7 p.m. we reached
Springfield, and after crossing over the "Little
Tugela" on a large and picturesque iron bridge, we
stopped a few moments to watch a large camp of
soldiers throwing up entrenchments close to their
tents, while others were swarming along the em-
bankments of the river, in nature's garb, thoroughly
enjoying the novelty of a good wash. We took a
snap-shot of the scene just as the sun was setting.

On we pushed, in spite of the fact that one of the
horses had almost given out. Some miles further

on we found out that the Naval Brigade had moved in the night, and were many miles ahead of us. That settled it. They had our tent, &c., so that we should have to sleep in the open or find a looted house. The latter turned up before long, and we soon felt quite at home. The place was beautiful, but in a complete state of wreckage; everything torn to pieces. We brought the waggon up close to the porch, and tied up the horses to a tree close by, so as to be in sight of looters. Then we gave the poor, tired, half-starved beasts a glorious feed of oat straw from the barns. The whole yard was covered with the straw stuff. Probably the soldiers who were feeding it to their horses had been suddenly called off.

We sat down to supper in a real dining-room; then, as the night was brilliant, we strolled down to the rushing river and made our dessert upon the pure atmosphere and the exquisite perfume of flowers, finishing off with a splendid wash, which so refreshed us that we quickly forgot our aching limbs and slept soundly.

Sunday, January 14th.—The sun streaming through the broken windows kissed us into wakefulness with a gentle reminder that we might expect a warm day. We rose accordingly, tumbled into the river, and thanked God that we were alive to enjoy all these good things. Even our usual bacon, hard tack, and coffee had a better flavour, whether because of our deeper content or superior appetite.

Carrying with us as much horse food as possible, we trekked away through lovely scenery lately in the occupation of the Boers, but now deserted, as they gradually yield to the impulse of the British army.

Our day's work was a trying one, comprising gullies, ruts, huge boulders, steep hills, and the most trying of fords. The effects of my recent illness were still heavy upon me, but having no leisure to nurse my symptoms I kept grimly on. Towards the end of the day I found myself gradually improving. Moral : Never give in to any ailment, and go in largely for pure air and an outdoor life. Some years ago I tramped through the Catskill Mountains without tent or night shelter of any kind except a blanket, and I was much surprised to see how quickly I got rid of a stubborn case of ulcerated sore throat.

The last climb was the worst, the naval guns were on the very top of a hill, which we made for without more ado. It was hard work to encourage our jaded beasts to carry us up to the camp, but we accomplished it at last, winding our way through endless numbers of tents. What a reception we did get ! Every tent was opened up, heads popped out, and everybody greeted us as if we had come back from the dead.

Here are some of the remarks which greeted us : " We were afraid you could not get here." " Have a drink." " Here, lads, gie us a hand to get their tent up." " Where will you roost ? " " My, that was plucky." Being by this time rather callous to possible dangers, I selected a spot for our tent under a shady tree a hundred feet behind the big 4.7 guns, consequently in line with the enemy's shells, if they decided to play with us. In fact every part of the hill was voted unsafe, but I thought that as we were close behind the brow of the hill the shots would pass over our heads and fall in the valley behind, which they did.

Captain Jones told me as soon as I arrived that I had a great treat in store, for the view from the gun position was wonderfully beautiful, and he had remarked to some one, " Well, I should just like to see Mr. Dickson's face when he first gets a look at it." No one would let me go on the hill until the evening's clear light, and then we had to crawl on all fours over the sky-line for fear the Boers should see us and locate our guns.

Never shall I forget my first impressions of this beautiful panorama. I could not tear myself away. Hour after hour I sat and gazed unappeased. Far down in the valley the silver Tugela wound, linking hills and mountains, until lost on the right and left of our encampment ; range after range of mountains passing beyond my vision until lost in the exquisitely tinted sunset clouds. The twilight falls and is succeeded by a full moon, imparting an indescribable sense of peace and beauty. What a contrast to what it may be to-morrow in the din of battle and crash of guns. Now there is nothing to be heard but the distant mellow cooing of the South African dove calling to its mate.

That night we held a veritable levee ; our tent was filled to overflowing, and we were overwhelmed with congratulations upon our safe return. We exchanged stories and drank toasts to our respective wives, sweethearts, and friends, and altogether gathered around us a distinct atmosphere of home. It was a pleasant evening, and we went to bed hoping that our dreams would be the continuation of our evening's events.

Monday, January 15th.—Shut up in our tent all day by the rain.

January 16*th.*—Scribbled and sketched up to
noon, when we were suddenly informed of a move.
We got our Biograph hastily into position between
and in front of the two big 4.7 guns located on the
brow of the hill. The position was too high to
admit of more than a panoramic view of the whole,
and our efforts moreover were hampered by the
descent of a severe rain storm which obliged us to
cover up the camera. We ourselves sat it out,
intent upon watching the thousands of troops going
out to meet the enemy. Our soldiers looked
wretchedly wet and bedraggled as they wound their
way over and around the kopjes. We could see
them slowly approach the river and test the crossing,
two men going up to their middles and wading
round to make sure that there were no entangle-
ments for the feet. Then the troopers followed one
by one, while others tried to engineer the ferry,
which they ultimately abandoned to our naval men,
the handy boys, who are signalled for from the
valley. Soon a party of thirteen was made up under
command of Lieutenant Chiazzari, with Chief
Gunner Instructor Baldwin assisting. They managed
to quickly repair the ferry and send the troops
across, toiling all evening and throughout the night
until dawn. General Buller sent word to Captain
Jones next morning that his men were worth their
weight in gold.

Baldwin's account of the feat is most entertaining.
I abbreviate it somewhat for convenience sake :
" We got orders to repair and handle the ferry just
as it was getting dark, so we nipped down the hill
and were soon at work, the Colonel of the Engineers
passing it over to us. Lieutenant Chiazzari took

the ferry while I remained on this side, and soon had the thing going in good shape. It's a wonder what a bit of rope will do along with plenty of willing chaps. We were six from the *Terrible*, and seven Natal Volunteers, including Lieutenant Chiazzari. As we were getting along smoothly, I sent a chap over to a looted house on the embankment to reconnoitre, light a fire and make tea. He soon came back and reported 'No wood.' I pumped him, and found out that the doors were still there. That settled the fire trouble, and when all was over we were able to get dried and fed. Before dawn we had taken nearly all over at the rate of 126 horses and three waggons in forty-two minutes, and this we repeated for two nights."

Wednesday, January 17th.—At 5 a.m. we hear a stentorian voice calling to us, "Get up, we shall soon be firing now. You'll be able to get hot water from the galley, and hurry breakfast." We were soon up and out, witnessing another fierce bombardment of the Boer fortifications and entrenchments. The night before our men had gallantly rushed the first Boer trenches, from which the enemy fled. The air is full of bursting shells, the Boer fortifications and upper trenches getting a terrific battering. At this rate we shall soon be able to occupy them—we hope.

We sat down close by the Biograph, not fifty feet from the big guns, and only ten feet below the brow of the hill, expecting every moment to see the flash of a Boer gun which might just as probably miss the naval guns and strike us.

The depth and vastness of the scene was so great as to somewhat disqualify it for a biographic view.

I fear very few will be able to discern the shells bursting, or the cavalry and artillery below us in the valley of the Upper Tugela. As for the foot soldiers in khaki, it will be quite impossible to see them, as they are always invisible from a distance, being the colour of the earth.

The exact position of our guns and those of the enemy can be seen by studying the accompanying panoramic sketch which was a laborious task.

PART OF A BIOGRAPH PANORAMA OF THE UPPER VALLEY OF THE TUGELA.

Every hill and dale and winding of the Tugela is shown, and should one see the Biograph panoramic projection of the valley at the time of the battle he will get a very good idea of the whole thing, even if the distant puffs should be invisible.

No rest is given our guns, the very earth seems to oscillate as we run to the Biograph, causing the strange and awful feeling akin to an earthquake. The scene was indescribably thrilling as we stood between two fires watching the smoke from the surrounding hills far and near, cannon and bursting shells.

General Warren's men got the worst of it on our left flank while engaging the enemy, but successfully driving them in towards us, while Lord Dundonald on our right doing the same, made a perfect trap for the Boers.

Thursday, January 18th, to Wednesday, 24th.—The doings of nearly a week can be summed up in our shelling the enemy, and endeavouring to dislodge them from their trenches. On the other side of Spion Kop to our left Sir Charles Warren's men are steadily fighting with the endeavour to drive the enemy towards us, when it will be our turn to pitch in. During this time of waiting we took the opportunity to visit the surrounding country, in the hope of being able to get our caravan nearer to Warren's forces; but being so hampered with our large camera and outfit I abandoned the project, trusting to get the battle in front of me. We therefore settled down to the repairing of our cart, foraging, and laying in what food there is to be found for this siege. We thought we were going right through to Ladysmith when we left Chieveley, but, alas, we discover that we have a formidable enemy, evidently greatly under-estimated in strength and stickativeness, and who moreover have the advantage of being upon familiar soil with advanced preparations for a long and desperate resistance.

A few days ago we were out foraging, and steered over towards the outposts to examine some ore beds, which tempted us rather dangerously near the enemy, obliging us to take turn and turn about watching while we sought samples for analysis.

Our lunch that day consisted of hard tack and peaches ; the fruit we discovered at a looted farm, a pretty home once occupied by British subjects, but shockingly devastated and now almost uninhabitable.

Last night Warren's forces recommenced the left flank attack on Spion Kop, and we received a message by a flag that they succeeded in getting

WE RECEIVED A MESSAGE BY FLAG.

halfway up the hill. All night long we listened to the deadly booming of gun and crackle of rifle, which hasn't yet ceased, twenty-four hours later. All night and all day they fought with only two slight intermissions for food—poor chaps. General Warren's plan is to drive the Boers into the plains below us here, while endeavouring to take the hills on his right as he advances. Meanwhile our guns are shelling right over Spion Kop, into the enemy on the other side, some shots being directed to the top, from which the enemy is firing both ways on Warren's men as they push their way up and on Spion Kop. As I now write I am watching men slowly climbing up the mountain. General Warren signals just now, " We are only just holding our own," upon which our big guns send shell after shell over the mountains and along the top, in the hope of scattering the enemy who are fighting with such dogged persistency.

Our guns on this hill are watching for Boers who may come from our right and cross the plain in order to reach their comrades on our left. I just happened to see a lot of them make a dash from out of some trees and bolt for another shelter, and as I was under one of the guns over the hillside, it didn't take me long to notify the commander, who whisked his field-glass in that direction, saw them, and ordered a lyddite shell to be sent in among them, with appalling results. So I suppose I must have some of that on my conscience, which, strangely enough, seemed to elate me rather than depress.

Thursday, 25th.—The battle rages on with unabated fury ; the slaughter on both sides is obliged to be terrible. All night long and far into the day there has been no cessation. The night before, our gunners were untiring in their efforts to help our boys by shelling the Boer position all along the Spion Kop ridges. Huge boulders could be seen crashing down into the valley below, loosened from the top and torn by our lyddite shells, narrowly missing our men who could be seen climbing up to hem in the Boers on the ridge. By morning three

BATTLE OF SPION KOP—AMBULANCE CORPS CROSSING THE TUGELA RIVER.

10

thousand of our braves had captured the mountain
and driven the Boers off. This would have been a
triumphant success had they been able to withstand
the deadly cross-fire of the enemy. There was no
shelter at all, poor chaps. They had stabbed their
way to a position which they hoped to hold, but
which they soon had to abandon or be utterly
annihilated. They had neither food nor water, and
so were ordered to retire. Some of the men were
seen crying with impotent rage and vexation in their
bitter disappointment.

We were not long in following with our Cape cart,
and after several hours' severe work for horse and
man succeeded in getting a good picture of the
Ambulance Corps crossing the Tugela River over a
hurriedly spanned pontoon bridge. In the immediate
foreground may be seen trenches filled with our men
to guard against any sudden attack should the
wounded be fired on by the enemy. A little below
the Tugela wends its way through great boulders
and a rocky bed, over which our sick and wounded
must be driven as they make their way down the
opposite side across the pontoon bridge and up the
embankment where we now are, the worse cases
being carried by innumerable volunteer stretcher-
bearers, mostly coolies.

On the other side, as far as the eye can reach the
Red Cross ambulances are seen waiting their turn
to make their perilous descent, nearly all of them
having been previously emptied of their worst cases
of wounded for fear of an upset, the patients being
carried over and replaced after arriving at the other
side, when comparatively on safe ground. The
picture has an additional value that in the back-

ground is part of the battlefield where Warren's
men fought so gallantly as they advanced towards
and up Spion Kop to the right.   We had no end of
difficulties in reaching our goal.   Just as we were
rounding a corner of the last camp in our valley a
messenger from the Provost Marshal overtook us to

AFTER THE BATTLE—CORTÈGES OF STRETCHER-BEARERS.

inquire into my papers, and twenty minutes of
valuable time had to be sacrificed in order to prove
that General Buller's permission covered our movements.

Another six miles and we found ourselves in a bog
hole, from which we extricated ourselves creditably

without harm to cart or horses. On the next rise were *cortèges* of stretcher-bearers extending over a distance of three or four miles. It was indescribably ghastly and heart-rending, and made me faint and sick at heart. I witnessed the passing away of two brave souls under fearful agony. Their bearers tenderly laid them down by the roadside.

Some of the wounded were smoking their pipes in the endeavour to alleviate their pain, but the distortion on their faces showed that the relief was slight. Half an hour later, just as we were descending the last long hill to the distant Tugela below, two officers rode up rapidly and stopping us, did their kindly best to dissuade us from going any further. All were ordered out of the valley, they said, as the Boers were momentarily expected to shell and cut the British forces off. Our Cape cart being so conspicuous, we should be a certain mark for the enemy. In addition to this, the officers pointed out a stream of artillery crossing the road and rapidly getting into position to meet the attack in the event of the Boers showing fight. This was my chance, I thought, and thanking the officers for their consideration, I drove on right into the midst of the field. We passed the artillery, who by that time were in position, their horses in the rear. Seeing no immediate signs of an attack, we drove a little further on and crossed a deep ravine, which was a herculean task for the horses inasmuch as we had to wait until a lot of artillery ammunition had passed through.

The liveliest scene awaited us on the bank of the river. Everybody was cross—no wonder, and so was I when told I couldn't take the picture. After I had consigned that particular officer to a warm place I proceeded with my work, then drove back to the artillery. I waited until the light grew too weak for photographing, then regretfully gave it up. As it was, however, the Boers did not attack the transports, but continued firing higher up, no shells reaching us. We had taken our lives in our hands hoping to get a biographic record from the flank, a feat

SOME OF THE WOUNDED FROM SPION KOP.

which would have been comparatively safe had we been dealing with civilised war tactics ; but it is impossible to trust to these treacherous Boers, who would relish shooting at a nice little side-show like our Cape cart.

I feel quite confident that General Buller's order, which was read aloud in all our camps, must have filtered through somehow to the Boers, as they appeared to profit by the information to murder many of our men under truce of their making. General Buller commanded (I heard the order) that the Boers were to be henceforth shot down when they showed the white flag, and that the British were not to cease firing until the enemy put down their rifles and raised their hands. This the Boers did yesterday, and as soon as our men had covered half the intervening distance in order to secure them as prisoners the Boers quickly stooped, seized their rifles and poured a most deadly fire into our ranks. Over seven hundred Boers are reported guilty of this dastardly piece of work. Up to the moment I write things seem going against us. We have had to give up the hills to the Boers and have lost over fifteen hundred men. As usual, there are many rumours accounting for the repulse.

I hardly ever remember spending such a horrible day; there seemed to be a general feeling abroad that our men were being uselessly sacrificed in thousands without bringing us any nearer to Ladysmith. Over three months have we been at it, and I cannot see how Ladysmith can hold out much longer. Of course the Boer slaughter has been considerable. Some of our men noticed 175 thrown into a trench for burial in one spot alone.

The thing which chiefly demoralised our men in this second edition of Majuba Hill was the fact that half the time they had to fire at nothing, so cleverly were the Boers hidden, while the British were being mowed down by rifle and cross-fire from the " doorknockers," or Maxim-Nordenfeldt repeating guns, making it quite impossible for our men to escape.

For some unaccountable reason, the British Government refused to take up this most deadly of all field weapons, and yet the Boers were allowed the entire use of them. If we had these guns with the one-pound explosive shells which the Boers use so effectively, one man wielding one as easily as a rifle, then I think Ladysmith would have been ours long ago. Our men shudder at the very sound, the moment they hear it ; and no wonder, for the accurate shooting accomplished with this murderous weapon is something fearful to see—men disembowelled, legs and arms carried away, and the ground torn to pieces.

Closely linked are the sublime and the ridiculous. The night preceding the above events had been filled with aggravating trivialities, all of which had combined to keep me awake. One of our party—I refrain from mentioning names—had kept up a loud and persistent snoring, and to this was added the maddening scratch, scratch, of a monster beetle which had been caught by one of my companions and shut up in a tin box preparatory to pickling. He got loose, of course, necessitating a long hunt in the dark. When found, I removed him and his tin to a position out of earshot. Nothing more unsettling to the nerves can be imagined than to move around at night barefooted, momentarily expecting to step on some live and gruesome thing. It was 2 a.m. when I disposed of the beetle ; meanwhile a gale had arisen, loosening the top tent cover, which flapped continuously for hours, until I got wild and reduced it to order. Thinking that my troubles were now over for the night, and hoping to secure a short interval of sleep, I turned over, when the cot suddenly lost foothold and landed me on the ground. After that I tried to sleep head down and feet up, but it was no good. Then our big guns commenced their deadly work, and through this, strangely enough, I slept until my pet kitten " Biograph " crawled all over me, playing tag to its heart's content and every now and again making a dash for my face. That settled it. I gave up sleeping as a bad job, and after joining Kitty in her pranks for a while, I got up, roused the others, and we fetched the mutograph from its elevated position on the hill; after which we packed it into the cart and trekked for the battle-field.

I forgot to mention in its proper connection that " Biograph " has a little history of her own. We found her in a deserted Kaffir kraal, abandoned to her fate. We carried her with us when we went to Chieveley, and there she remained a while until she was appropriated by one of the camps. We had not long to mourn her loss, however, for she was brought back by a sailor who had seen her in our tent. Rather than risk losing her again I made her a collar, and wrote on it: " Biograph is my name. Please take me home." Twice she was lost, and twice brought back. Once when we were trekking we had to fasten Kitty to the outer wickerwork of a lime-juice bottle ; indeed she has had many strange receptacles. Wherever we are, the little thing is a perfect comfort. Many an officer and soldier has stopped at our tent " just for a taste of home," and have found it difficult to tear themselves away from the little pet. " Biograph " is a distinct feature in our household.

Friday, January 26th.—We spend an uncomfortable day, physically and mentally; physically in much pain, and mentally disgusted at the unexpected turn everything has taken. The Boers are in full possession of the hills on our left flank, while our men have all returned across the Tugela in a bitter state of disappointment. This inaction is inevitable, of course, but it is maddening to think that the Boers meanwhile are getting comfortably entrenched and effecting junctions with their companions.

Saturday, 27th, to Monday, 29th.—All quiet. Still waters run deep; a calm before a storm. It is rumoured that General Buller says we will get into Ladysmith by Sunday. He harangued the regiments on the subject of how to take advantage of the rocky, natural covers, so as not to expose themselves unnecessarily to the fire of the enemy, and wound up with the encouraging statement above mentioned. Pouring rain and all sick, including horses. We must grin and bear it.

Upper Valley of the Tugela, February 2, 1900.— The Boers are determined that we shall not get through and relieve Ladysmith, and we are having a time of it. We commenced with Colenso and had to give it up, after putting forth our best efforts during more than a month's siege; then we decamped and tried the other side, with much the same results. I fear there will be much loss of life before we can reach our goal. History repeats itself. The war of 1881 bears a good deal of similarity to recent events. I quote from a history of the Transvaal:

"War broke out on December 13, 1880. The English population, which, depending on the promises of the Government, had flocked into the country, were beleaguered in different towns, and a small force under Colonel Anstruther was almost annihilated at Bronkhorst Spruit. It was, however, on colonial territory that our most humiliating defeats were experienced. General Sir George Colley, then Governor of Natal, and Commander-in-chief of the Forces, marched to the relief of the beleaguered town with a small army of 1,000 men. His progress was arrested by a Boer commando under Joubert. On attempting to force the passage at Laing's Nek on the 28th of January, 1881, Colley was driven back to his camp on Mount Prospect with heavy loss. On the 7th of February another crushing reverse was experienced on the Ingogo Heights. After a fortnight's delay, during which reinforcements arrived, Colley, with 600 men, executed that amazing ascent of Majuba Hill. His position was attacked at dawn, on the 27th of February, by a small party of Boers ; and nearly half the British force, which ran short of ammunition, were killed or wounded in the panic which ensued.

" Colley, whatever his capabilities as a General may have been, met his death like a soldier whilst endeavouring to bring his men to the charge. Only one of the Boers was killed ; their loss in the three engagements barely exceeding a dozen men. We can well understand that their predicant, in his thanksgiving sermon, should take for his text : ' The sword of the Lord and of Gideon.'

" This action practically closed the war, and the reinforcements which arrived were never used. Peace was concluded as soon as possible, and the

Government of the South African Republic was again formally recognised."

This General Joubert is an astute and far-sighted man, and I doubt not has long since planned the details of the present battle, familiar as he is with every mountain fastness and natural fortification.

Instead of a thousand or so of men we have eighty thousand, and of these nearly forty thousand are pre-

TUGELA RIVER.

paring to fight to-morrow. Every valley and low hill-side invisible to the enemy is occupied by our people. Some poor chaps in the valley below have been for eighteen days lying in the open without tent or protection of any kind. They were ordered to creep over to the first ridge or kopje in the centre of the plain and keep in hiding, so that if the Boers attempted to take the situation they could be effectually resisted. And now, little by little, our troops are being brought around to the front in order to concentrate their forces for an early *grand coup*.

Our small party took a trip across the Tugela valley, and on our return delayed a while to enjoy a swim in the river, and to collect from its bed a variety of precious stones. We found many opals, onyx, and beautiful crystals, which some day may lose their rough exterior through the skill of the lapidary. How our men do enjoy a good wash! I took some snap-shots, showing a portion of the riverside encrusted with Tommies washing their clothes, &c.

Sunday, February 4*th.*—The battle was to have been fought to-day, but the General has promised that it shall take place to-morrow instead. All are jubilant. It makes me proud to hear the plucky chaps swearing, with flashing eyes, to "raise hell with the brutes," and to punish them for their lost comrades. Not a thought of self and the horrors with which they are about to deal. The only thing which seems to depress them is the invisibility of the enemy, while they are for ever in the open field getting murdered with shell and rifle from above.

This is the eve of the great battle. Could our friends at home see these long ranges of mountains rising precipitously towards the clouds, and realise how effectually these same mountains guard the approach to Ladysmith, their first thought would be that we should never get through.

By way of diversion we all rode to Springfield, five miles distant, to arrange for an artillery picture. On our return we got into a bog, and nearly lost a horse, besides being splashed from head to foot.

February 5th, 5 a.m.—The battle rages. Guns are being fired from the hills to cover our men's advance. We dress hastily, and get ready to view or photograph the conflict from Eagle's Crag. Our naval guns are doing their best to silence our enemy's long-reaching guns, which are stationed to

OUR NAVAL GUNS ARE DOING THEIR BEST TO SILENCE OUR ENEMIES'
LONG-REACHING GUNS.

our left near Spion Kop. There is another gun high up on Doornkloof, and well out of our reach. Our cavalry and artillery are getting a large number of shells which, strangely enough, do but little harm, although it is difficult to see how the men escape, as they never swerve from their position, but stand unflinchingly by the guns. The shells explode around them in immense numbers, but the men do not even turn their heads to see the result. It is impossible to speak too highly of their bravery. The plan of attack is specially directed towards drawing the enemy's fire so as to be able to locate the position of the Boers and their guns with exactitude. It is then proposed to withdraw. This having been accomplished before nightfall, our infantry, who had advanced to the Boer lines, returned the enemy's fire with interest for several hours, slowly retreating the while, but not until they had rescued a gun which had been disabled by the enemy's shell. This they coolly manned and dragged off the field under severe fire, each man laying hold of the long ropes and pulling by main force. One wheel was blown off during the rescue. While this was going on the Boers were amusing themselves by firing on a row of Red Cross tents at the foot of Swartkop, destroying two, which necessitated a quick change of position under the shelter of the hill. Our cavalry, while waiting in the open for orders, were cruelly shelled, and forced to seek cover for a while. To-day's fighting lies principally to the right of the valley; to-morrow our men are to storm the row of kopjes.

Last night we caught a spy crawling up on hands and knees to our guns, in order, I suppose, to discover how many we had and where placed. He was soon disposed of.

No news from home for four weeks, as we are shut off from the telegraph, and everything has to go through the censor's hands. Often we do not even know what happens around us. The statements of the war correspondents are very much overhauled, and only portions of the truth are allowed to go through.

February 6th and 7th.—After a night of wakefulness and discouragement we recommence shelling at dawn, while our infantry make a rush for the kopjes on our right front. Before night we have gained three-quarters of the ridges. Meanwhile the artillery has advanced far over towards the enemy in support of our men, amid showers of shells. This we secured biographically from our hill, noting the dignified and orderly retreat of the artillery. The infantry's fire from both sides is blended into a continuous roar, so incessant is the firing. We made an attempt to get down with our heavy apparatus among the shells, but had to give it up until I could hire a team of oxen, which I did next day (7th).

This morning (7th), at 3.15, we pulled our tent down and packed everything up, expecting that the guns would be planted on the lower kopjes near the river to the right. Just as we were ready to go Captain Jones came to us in the dark, saying, "The General has countermanded his order, and we stay." So we had to do without our tents that day, expecting hourly to trek. Had we proceeded to the new position we should most likely all have been murdered, as the spot intended for our guns was within easy reach of those of the enemy. This we noted during the day's fighting.

Our domestic conditions are rather uncomfortable. We are stretched out under the trees without shelter, lying on our cots and making the best of it on empty stomachs. The men of the Naval Brigade who are in the same plight were relieved just now by kind-hearted Captain Jones, who ordered breakfast to be made in the hope that the command to trek would not come. We followed the example of the lads and fell to upon bully beef and hard tack, washed down with tea.

Our losses were extremely slight yesterday, and very few were injured to-day. Our men have gained possession of almost all the Krantzkloof kopjes, and are holding them splendidly.

One of my companions is down with some kind of fever, and cannot move hand or foot, so we are shorthanded. If we could only get to sleep at night I think we should all feel better ; but what with the bellowing cattle and talkative Kaffirs, the occasional visits from our horses who try to enter the tent, and the sudden and violent showers of rain, our cup of misery is full. By noon we managed to get off and down the hillside with our paraphernalia, but it was impossible to go any further down the precipitous road leading to the lower valley by any ordinary methods of locomotion. After an hour's hard work we succeeded in tying up the wheels, and slid down the most incredibly rough and steep descent. On our return we may be able to hire a team of oxen to pull us back. My companions insisted on going with me, so anxious were they to see the battle a little nearer, and I gave in, much against my better judgment. We arrived without accident at the foot of the mountain, but there my companions caved in. I thought at first it might be sunstroke, owing to the burning heat, and after unhitching the horses I made the boys as comfortable as possible under the cart, after which I managed to make some tea, which partially revived them. Shells were bursting all around us, and thinking that in this case certainly the better part of valour was prudence, I made my preparations to get away under shelter of the base of the hill. Hitching up, I drove on, skirting the hills as closely as possible so as to keep out of the enemy's sight. I left the sickest man resting in a donga in charge of the Cape cart, while I went on with the other to find a spot for the camera.

We gradually pushed our way along the hill and riverside, to emerge finally on the plain, crawling on hands and knees and taking advantage of every large boulder, until we reached the Boers' deadly fire. Just in front of us our artillery were receiving shell after shell, but not a movement did they make.

While I was intently watching our men a soldier, standing at my side, jumped behind my boulder, shouting, " Look out, here she comes. Just then I heard the six-inch Boer guns roar, but having previously timed the landing of the shells, I knew I had two or three seconds' time to get a snap—which I did, then dived behind the rock followed by a sound so terrible that it is enough to make one's blood curdle—the bursting of a six-inch melinite shell at close range. The moment I heard the explosion I was up and snapped it. This I repeated several times ; then, as the shells were bursting within two hundred yards of our rock and things were getting altogether too hot to be pleasant, I crawled back—not, however, before I had snapped the position I was in, for the sake of the unbeliever.

Getting back to a safer position, we watched the valiant attack of our men as they gradually pushed on. Had we had a light camera these movements could have been secured, and many others of an invaluable nature, but the enormous bulk of our apparatus which had to be dragged about in a Cape cart with two horses, prevented our getting to the spot. The difficulties were aggravated by· the absence of roads, while the huge gullies we had to cross and the enormous boulders we had to get over made the enterprise almost impracticable. We really risked our lives to secure the views, but finding it impossible to drag our machine into position,

SOLDIERS FILLING THEIR WATER BOTTLES WHILE THE BATTLE RAGED.

we returned to where we had left our horses and sick man. They had vanished. Two hours later, just as night was coming on, we found the caravan and invalid at the foot of the hill. The sick man was half delirious. I undid the horses, made an impromptu saddle of a sack filled with straw, and sent him on, leaving Cox helplessly sick inside the cart, while I rode on after Seward for fear he should fall off. It was then very dark, and we had to trust entirely to our horses picking their way among the huge boulders. Twice only did my horse fall—not a bad record when you take into consideration the cacti, rocks, gullies, and bear-holes between which they had to tread. I reached camp shortly after Seward, only to find him half-conscious and in great pain. After getting him to bed, I hunted out a brave Kaffir boy and told him to carry Cox his blankets and some food, directing the lad to remain all night with the cart. That night it had unfortunately happened that no password had been received in our camp, so there was nothing for me to do but to write a note of explanation on my business card, hoping that if the Kaffir were arrested the officer in charge would know me—and so it happened ; the Kaffir giving me next day an animated account of his being held up and interrogated, then being finally allowed to go on and carry out his mission.

Thursday, February 8th.—I rose at dawn and made breakfast, did what I could for Seward, then departed on horseback to Cox, leading the other horse. After two and a half hours of hard work pushing my way through the retreating forces, I reached the foot of the hill where I had left the cart and Cox the night before, and found that gentleman a mere pulp, unable to stir hand or foot. He had been kept awake all night by retreating soldiers who stumbled over the cart shaft at intervals. Before long we were again the recipients of a little Boer attention in the shape of shells aimed at our troops and convoy. These narrowly missed us. A soldier assisted us to dig up some of the fragments for the edification of our people at home.

After some difficulty I succeeded in getting a span of twelve oxen to help our horses pull up the hills, and had it not been for this most timely assistance, which we owed to Mr. J. H. Muir, we should doubtless have had to spend another night in the valley without the slightest protection. As it was we got in before dark, and I was exhausted enough by that time to be ready for bed. First, however, I had to make supper, feed the horses, &c., &c., our Kaffir having long since forsaken us.

February 9th and 10*th*.—My patients are delirious at intervals, and I shall have to risk taking them through to Frere in the Cape cart, a twelve-hour trek. The Naval Brigade surgeon, Dr. Lilly, fears it may be enteric fever, and thinks we should push on as quickly as possible; so I must face the journey unassisted. I completed my packing as rapidly as possible in order to trek with the Brigade, who are returning to Springfield for the first stop. When I had finished and hitched up the horses, which were unusually restive that morning, I bundled my sick men into the cart, Seward lying out in a dead faint, while Cox sat beside me with his head tied up and looking absolutely ghastly. I drove down the hillside as quickly as possible so as to catch up with the waggons and guns, which had got far ahead of us. Our friends of the navy had very kindly consented to take nine-tenths of our things to the first railroad station, so that I could have a little more room in the cart for my sick. What an indescribably horrible night we had, trekking alone and in the dark over the wide and almost pathless veldt; no stop from 6 p.m. to 9 a.m. the next morning. My plan was to catch the morning train from Frere, which was a through mail to Durban.

Just before reaching the first bad drift near Springfield we caught sight of the rear van of the Naval Brigade, which I hailed to deposit the sick in so that I should not get stuck in the drift. I then drove the cart through with voice and whip, just managing to get out after sticking twice. After plunging through the mud and water interspersed with huge boulders, I was confronted by the almost perpendicular sides of the gully. Further along I came to a group on the road, to find Seward in another dead faint and on his last legs, it seemed. With some assistance from one of the sailors who had remained behind to await my coming, we got Seward into the cart and pushed on by starlight. Soon after we reached Springfield, where the Naval Brigade stopped for the night. After feeding my patient with Liebig's Extract mixed with cold water, I pushed on as soon as the horses had finished their oats, followed by warm wishes and sympathetic words. Our thoroughbreds did their work well up and down hill, through fords, &c., &c. Twenty times during the journey I was obliged to crawl on hands and knees looking for a particular faint wheel track which I knew led in the direction of Frere; besides this I was guided by the Southern Cross, the relation of which to my destination I had noted. Occasionally we would stop a moment for light refreshments; Liebig, condensed milk and water for the invalids, while I feasted on bully beef. The beef was overrun with myriads of ants, but I had long since got accustomed to such small deer.

I was soon to be rewarded for all my troubles by the sight of a glorious sunrise. As I trudged faintly at the head of the horses I began to see the road a little more clearly. Day was approaching, and with it renewed strength. Presently the sun rose, setting fire to the fleecy clouds surrounding the east, and bringing with it a sense of companionship and comfort in the lonely vastness. I could reply now with greater confidence to the incessant question, "How far are we now?" that we were then almost within sight of the promised land.

At 8 a.m., just as we were going to cross the last ford one of the horses got his hind-foot over the bar, and finding it rather restful, deliberately sat down on it, gradually finding his way to the ground, where he remained quietly making his breakfast from such bunches of grass as were within easy reach. When I argued with him he only neighed, remarking, I suppose, that he was having a good feed and rest and had no idea of moving.

Just then some of Colonel Templar's men came up, and between us we got started again. Colonel Munroe, of the Seaforth Highlanders, met me and was quick to see what had happened. In less than five minutes he had called up the medical staff, stretcher-bearers and orderlies; but after talking it all over we decided to stick to my first plan, which was to rush through to Durban and get into the sanatorium, where the sick men could receive the best of attention from the medical experts and nuns, besides change of air and scene. Throughout this whole campaign Colonel Munroe has been our good genius. I told him jokingly that he always made his appearance when we were in a tight place. I was speaking of him once to some men, and one of them remarked, "There's many an officer could take a hint from him in kindly courtesy ; there's no man better liked."

Stationmaster Hanson and his wife did all they could to help us, and we were soon speeding away on the train towards Durban. There was no possibility of getting breakfast anywhere, so I resorted to the ants and bully beef, washed down with condensed milk and water, while my companions laid out on the seats, tossing and moaning with pain and taking occasional doses of Liebig. At Maritzburg the military officers tried to pull Seward off his bed and carry him on their stretchers to the hospital. After several futile attempts, finding us firmly opposed to their measures, we were left alone.

After another twelve hours of travel we reached Durban, where we received every attention from the stationmaster, Mr. Irons. He telephoned first to the distant sanatorium to announce our coming and then saw us off in our rickshaws, taking charge of my horses and baggage. As soon as my companions were ensconced in bed, with the Sisters in attendance, I felt I had the right to collapse, which I did, sleeping soundly until daylight, a custom I had fallen into in camp. However tired I might be, I used invariably to wake at dawn with the booming of the guns.

Sunday, February 11*th*.—What a haven of rest ! I am taking my full share of the good things, and remained in bed trying to get over my extreme exhaustion ; only until after breakfast, however, which was deliciously prepared by one of the Sisters. The nuns, by the way, are mostly French Bretons. I found my companions very ill, and after a little consultation with the Lady Superior we phoned for the enteric specialist, Dr. Dumas, who reported Seward up to 105.6°, and Cox 103.5°. Not a bad start! I don't know if it will be my turn next, but I doubt extremely if I shall be ill, since I took every precaution in camp never to touch water if I could possibly avoid it, while Seward, poor fellow, drank all he could beg, borrow or steal—result enteric.

Before leaving our camp I arranged with some friends to wire me when my presence was needed for biographing purposes ; so now I shall rest quietly for a few days. I have secured the services of a strong chap to handle the camera whenever I make my next advance. A word about the sanatorium, and then to bed. We are situated high above the city and bay, which lie at our feet, bearing a strong resemblance to Naples. Our windows command this exquisite view and give us the best of air to breathe. The little nuns are untiring in their gentle ministrations ; unobtrusive, yet always ready with some kindly act or helpful word. I heard them singing this morning as I lay in bed. Theirs is no life of sloth and inaction.

February 12*th* to 16*th*.—As yet I have received no despatch from the front, and must wait with as much patience as I can muster. As I write this by candle-light in my room the air is filled with groans and cries. On my right some poor soul is talking away for dear life, another at the end of the passage is singing something distantly resembling a hymn. My patients are not improving, and now we fear Cox is in for enteric as well. Poor boys ! I shall be forced to leave them soon if there are any signs of Ladysmith being relieved. This sanatorium is full of enteric patients; the nuns have made a speciality of nursing those who have caught this insidious and awful fever, and the physicians in attendance are experts in this line of work.

Frere Station, February 21, 1900. — And so I must leave the ill men in the best of hands at the Durban Sanatorium, carefully watched and tended day and night ; arranging that should anything go wrong, they will quickly recall me from the front.

After considerable difficulty I succeed in finding a workman who professes to be tired of life, and doesn't care a rap where he goes.   On these grounds I employ him, and we start for Chieveley the same evening at 5.40, arriving next morning, after a sleepless night, in rather a disordered frame of mind from having been wakened so often for either railway or military passes at various stations.   On reaching Mooi River a suspect was turned out of his comfortable bunk to spend the remainder of the night on the platform.   His pass was not satisfactory, it seemed.   We had all noted his extreme reticence and lack of politeness throughout the trip ; and I regret to have to record an entire absence of sorrow at his misfortune.

February 22nd.—At dawn we reached Frere, and discovered that Mr. David Hunter and his railroad engineers were in the next car, going through to Colenso in order to plan for the reconstruction of the bridge. This decided me to remain on board and push through to the terminus of the line, as this was the first mail train that had ventured that far. I could not consent to miss this little bit of excitement.

Soon we left Chieveley, and were steaming along, not without some caution, towards the Boer-infested hills of Colenso. We passed a large body of cavalry commanded by Lord Dundonald ; they were just visible in the grey dawn. This added spice to the run. Slowly we approached the station, where we were met by the kind-hearted but doleful station-master, Milne, who invited us to breakfast. This we had to cut short owing to the overpowering stench caused by the remains of a horse which the Boers had driven into the waiting-room and shot, for our special benefit it would seem. Although Mr. Milne's house, or what remained of it, was two hundred yards off from this pest, we could not endure it, and so we made a rush to the river, not, however, before our kind host, who had evidently become somewhat accustomed to the awful combination of carbolic and dead horse, had shown us around his premises to see the way in which the Boers had ruthlessly destroyed everything ; adding insult to injury by the innumerable scrawls on the walls in Dutch and broken English which were in no way complimentary.

On crossing a deserted camp we found our men had been reading the account of my doings with the Biograph during this campaign, and had left scattered about a hundred or more copies of the *Natal Witness* open at the article referring to this. Curious that I should have arrived on this field precisely on the day of the publication of this number of the paper.

While wandering about over the Colenso battle-field, we came across large numbers of broken shell, shrapnel, and other relics of a terrific tussle. On returning to the station we were in time to experience once more the disagreeable sound of shells flying over our heads.

The Boers had fired their range-finding shells, and momentarily we expected to be bombarded. They, however, devoted their time to shelling our troops to the right as they advanced between kopjes. I can imagine nothing more demoralising than the bursting of these shells; it is the most painful sight to the looker-on. I needed no glasses to see every movement made, and was glad the order for retiring was given for the time. A gap or two had been made by the shells, and when the men had retired our Red Cross department was already at work in small bunches. After a short delay, which I think was done to throw the Boers off the scent, a rush was made. The guns roared as our men disappeared around a kopje, and so I lost sight of them.

Returning to the station, I found it packed with dying and wounded, lying on stretchers ready to be put on the train, while Red Cross waggons were full, waiting their turn to do the same.

I had enough, I thought, for that day, and I hung on to a freight train and returned to Chieveley, being just in time to witness the handcuffing of a brutal type of negro who had killed three of our men. He had been caught red-handed, after which he then murdered his two keepers. It is quite an unusual thing for the Kaffirs to be anything but friendly. At this time several low-type Boers were brought in, all of whom, of course, had to submit to being photographed as they were made to pose at the windows of the train.

My venerable and kindly companion of the morning was the Rev. Father Fullis, who had been sent for to bury some dead of his faith. I was deeply interested in the stories he told me of his experiences.

The firing had again commenced, and, like an old war-horse, I cannot keep away from the powder. Seeing the armoured train ready for a dash, I climbed in with the engineer and stoker, and off we went carrying 400 Imperial Light Infantry men. An early Biograph picture shows the kind of open cars they use, slitted at regular intervals through which to fire. The engine itself has since been covered with matting of huge ropes. The Biograph shows how they did it. I had to return almost immediately as I had no horse and was dependent on the trains, one of which was just going back to take General Wolf Murray and some railroad engineers, and also Father Fullis. We were all in an open car, and had a good opportunity of seeing the country and what was going on. It was a wonder we were not shelled, as the enemy had previously found the range. After wishing the General good-night I got off at Frere, and as long as it was light continued making every preparation to drive on next day early.

That night we were regaled by a soldiers' concert of the very best; bright spontaneous humour pre-vailed; clever impromptu songs and dances; a gramophone was handled very well by an officer; the accompaniments were played by the landlord's daughter. The piano had been hauled out on the porch, and the little intervening space between the little inn and the store covered over. All was bright and happy, and the war was forgotten for a time.

February 23rd.—Before leaving Frere I made the round of the field hospitals, and was delighted to see how well the sick were cared for; British and Boer getting the same attention.   In one tent three Boers lay side by side chatting; two were getting well, while the third looked ghastly, having been shot through the liver.   I talked for some time with them in German, endeavouring to draw them out in their opinion regarding the war.   They expressed themselves as being most anxious to be done with it all and return to their homes.   As we were passing into another tent we heard a poor chap call out to the doctor who was accompanying me, " I'm done," and on being questioned, said that " Jimmy over there being off his head got out of bed, and knowing it would kill him I crawls out and gets him back again, when I feels a great pain—oh, I'm done ! " This is a touching instance of the noble unselfishness of our men.   The chap had perhaps given his life to save his friend ; both had enteric, and every precaution had been taken to keep them quiet.

Before leaving this neighbourhood I visited the 6-in. naval gun, a veritable monster, whose projectiles carried ten miles with deadly effect, and whose roar shook the very ground for miles.   Fortunately I did not have to follow in the wake of this larger gun ; I found the 4.7 guns quite large enough.

February 26th.—I am lost in admiration over the stoical manner in which our men suffer and joke over it all.   To-day I photographed the men as they were being carried from the Red Cross waggons to the trains at Colenso.   Before they were lifted out I went from waggon to waggon telling them about the Biograph, and how their friends at home would see them, and that they must put the best foot forward. Although suffering severely they were cheery, and amused themselves chaffing with each other.   The stretcher-bearers fell in with my idea and gave me every assistance, and soon a lot of them on stretchers, carried on each other's backs, &c., were ready to march past the machine, one fellow remarking as he tried to rise, " Hello, old chap, are you winding us up for another go at old Krooger ? "

Shortly after we had finished, the enemy commenced shelling us again, knowing that we were trying to get the ambulance trains loaded. It was very hard and trying work indeed for all ; the wounded and dying, mute in their agony, only looked at us as though saying, " For God's sake get me out of the hot sun and away." One poor man I had been watching for some time paled and died without a word. A shell narrowly missed the train shed, and buried itself two hundred yards beyond. Many are now leaving, as the place is within range of shot, and we may get it hot at any moment. (The same evening the shelling began.)

But we are hungry, thirsty, and greatly fatigued, and in spite of the shells we accept Messrs. Playfair, Ewing, and Smith's kind offer to make us a cup of tea, their tent being close at hand. These gentlemen, let me add, devote their whole time and energy to a life of use among the Tommies, providing them with personal comforts of every kind, and often, from what I hear, they have encouraged many a poor fellow who had to let go his hold of Mother Earth. Mr. Ewing, who accompanied us in our Cape cart back to camp, shared our excitement of being most unmercifully shelled while in our company. We had no sooner rounded a kopje and were crossing an open plain, stopping for a moment to collect some curios, when we were rather rudely

awakened to the fact that we had been sighted.   I
was exceedingly anxious to get a shell, but consideration for the welfare of all made me give up
the quest.   Just then, with an ever-increasing sound
which makes the cold chills run down my back at
the mere recollection of it, a huge 100-pound Creusot
shell *narrowly* missed the top of my Cape cart and
buried itself twenty yards beyond.   The enemy had
evidently found the range, and the next, doubtless,

COLONEL LONG'S ARTILLERY HORSES, BATTLE OF COLENSO.

would finish things up for us before we could reach
Ladysmith ; so deeming flight the better part of
valour, I whipped up and tore pell-mell in a zigzag
across the open, not, however, before I had collected
some of the harness and shells found around Colonel
Long's artillery horses.   I had been told at one time
never to run straight when under fire.   By tacking
about they are prevented from firing with any
accuracy.   We had a few moments of suspense

while trying to get over a muddy crossing or gully.

I have often wondered at the manner in which our horses stand under fire, never flinching even, and sometimes wandering within a few feet of the guns while grazing, with a careless indifference to their surroundings. The battle rages all around us ; the Boers fleeing from shell and bayonet before the smoke of a shell from our guns has blown away. Our Tommies can be seen making a rush among them and driving them out of their trenches, while giving them cold steel to their heart's content, howling and cheering them as they prod them, saying "Take that for Jimmy, and that for my mate, you swine !" Grobler's Kloof, &c., all had a bloody history, as well may be seen from the number of dead and wounded which were carried through the hospitals, an ever sad and painful sight.

February 27*th*.—The road is clearing rapidly, and soon now we shall be able to get through to Lady-smith. Our naval men, as usual, have been crowning themselves with glory. General Buller, at a critical moment, wanted the big guns moved silently within a few hours, in the dead of night, to an adjoining hill, so as to open fire on the enemy at dawn as a little surprise, and so effectually complete the rout. It was done, and, as an eye-witness, I must say it was a marvellous feat. The hill was reported inaccessible, but Captain Jones and Commander Limpus, who have never stopped for anything, gave the order, and it was executed. When asked by a staff officer if it could be done, he was quietly answered in the affirmative, so sure was the Commander of his men under the direct superintendence of Chief Baldwin. Thus at dawn, after the herculean task, the guns were doing their deadly work, and the day was ours. Afterwards we were pushing on, sleeping in our cart, without tent or other shelter, under a pouring rain.

The cool bravery of our British soldiers cannot better be exemplified than by an incident in Commander Limpus's career here. Two or three days ago he was sitting close to one of the 4.7 guns which was under heavy fire. A shell landed between the gun and where he was sitting watching the result of his last shot. He never took his eyes off his glasses, and as soon as the dust had partially cleared he called out, still without moving, " Number one gun's crew, is there any one hurt ? " and the cry came back as dispassionately, " No one hurt, sir." " Train a little to the right."

March 1st.—At dawn we find ourselves close to the Tugela again, very wet, but very happy at the glorious news that the road is clear through to Ladysmith. Now here's a chance for our splendid stallions to make a record. We must push through and get in on this the first day—and we did, but we nearly killed the horses and ourselves. My new assistant is a sailor (sufficient recommendation for me, I thought), but alas ! as the days wore on I discovered that he had a horror of horses, and whenever mine plunged and reared, pawing the ground, or fighting with each other, he fled for his life, assisting me at such times by doing all or a large percentage of the swearing, meanwhile running round and round the brutes at a safe distance, while I, being so convulsed with laughter at his antics, was hardly

able to keep the animals in check. For two days I
had to nurse this poor fellow and do everything
myself, while he lay on his back in great agony from
one of his periodical attacks of sciatica, during which
time he kept the atmosphere all around him blue. I
may some day discover great things in him ; at present he only keeps me in a gale of laughter from
morning till night. He has brought a lot of writing-
paper, envelopes, pens and ink, hoping to sell at a
small profit. I must of course give in and let him
go across to his old crew on a time limit of
twenty minutes to sell his stuff, half of which he
took with him. Little did I think that I should turn
salesman on his behalf during his absence. An
officer passed me at the time and, taking in the
situation, he roared with laughter.

The well-built pontoon bridge lay before us as I
waited my turn to cross. I was allowed to wedge
my cart in between some artillery and transport
waggons, and so got over without mishap, being
greeted on every side by the officers wanting to know
if I was going to get through to-day. I could only say
I hoped to do so, not knowing what other difficulties
lay in my way. It is well I didn't know, for I think
I might have been tempted to take two days instead
of driving through that day. We pushed on up hill
and down dale, getting ahead at every possible
chance when the road was wide enough to drive in
front of the thousands of waggons, &c. Finally
we caught up with our naval friends encamped upon
a large open plain, together with the rest of the
troops. Here was the limit. A mile beyond the
river was seen in another of its windings, and Ladysmith lay ten miles or more from the point around
the crossing.

THE ROAD IS CLEAR THROUGH TO LADYSMITH—PONTOON BRIDGE.

I was told no civilian would be allowed to enter
Ladysmith on this day, and that an armed cordon
had been placed around the town. In spite of the
cordial invitation to rest and join in a very tempting
feast, we pushed on, intending to eat on the way.
Soon, however, we were stopped and subjected to
inquiries. Fortunately, I was able to plead my
cause in person to the Provost-Marshal, who just then
rode up. He had been strictly enjoined by General
Buller and General Warren to prevent any un-
authorised ingress. I succeeded in persuading him
to hunt up General Buller, but as he was not to be
found the Provost galloped all over the grounds
in search of General Warren. Thanking Major
Chichester for his trouble we drove on, and were
soon trying to ford a discouragingly deep and rapid
river. Many essayed the crossing unsuccessfully,
and all gave it up as being too risky. To go
around would throw us back several hours, but there
was no help for it, so we turned our backs discon-
solately on Ladysmith and drove along the river for
about two and a half miles, where we found a bridge
and effected a crossing by the help of some Kaffirs,
who pushed us up the opposite embankment. There
we recommenced our difficult task, tumbling over
huge boulders up and along the side of Umblewana.
The worst part lay between the bridge and the deep
crossing. The horses, though much worn, struggled
on bravely. They tackled every rise successfully
until the last, and when halfway through that they
gave way, discouraged largely through the pouring
rain. The cart backed downhill in a most alarming
manner ; huge rocks and boulders on one side, and
nothing on the other to prevent the whole affair

from rolling over the precipice into the river or valley below. I just managed in time to throw the horses around so that one of the wheels caught in the rocks, where it struggled for a moment to recover its balance. With great caution I succeeded in turning round, my sure-footed beasts scrambling sideways through young Gibraltars. There was not a soul on the road to help push, so we decided to give it up and try some other path of a less slippery description. I gave the head of one of the horses to the care of my sciatica-afflicted companion, while I led the other, and with the aid of a decrepit old Kaffir, who had just then come up, we made another effort to reach the top, which meant Ladysmith for us that night. With whip on my side and curses on my companion's, we got to the top after a mad race, only just succeeding in reaching the flat of a Kaffir kraal. The starved beasts proceeded to demolish one of the huts as a solace to their ravenous appetites, while we lay in the wet grass panting with exhaustion. After paying a trifle for the injured hut we proceeded on our journey. Soon afterwards we found ourselves on the opposite shore from the ford which we had failed to make, and a little further on we are on what was once Boer land, and had we been provided with waggons we could have taken much food, such as it was, to the people of Ladysmith, besides tents and other camping things.

On reaching the lower end of Umblewana, we paused a moment on a slight eminence to view the little town, which we could see far away across the open plain close to the opposite hills. To our left, just discernible in the waning light, we could see a

large camp.   It was then we realised what a terrible
time they must have had to be bombarded day and
night, an open target for Long Tom, which had
been for so many months settled on Umblewana
heights.   In a pouring rain we reached the plain,
and sought the long disused road among the high
grass.   It is a curious fact that this road was so

WE GET INTO LADYSMITH.

entirely obscured by the tall grass that it was difficult to find.   No one had used it or could use it for
months.   As we approached the town we were
besieged by hungry men, and soon everything we
had went ; we just keeping enough for supper and
breakfast, trusting to the provision waggons getting
in next day.   It was then pitch dark, and not

knowing into what awful pitfalls I might plunge, I persuaded a scout to ride in front and in the best part and give us fair warning should anything be in the way. Soon we came to a halt, and had to drive around huge stone walls barricading the road. We found many of these at varying distances, which proved most interesting when seen later by daylight.

In another hour, after driving from door to door for a bed, we were forced to settle down at the railway hotel among indescribably bad smells of putrid flesh ; in fact the whole town and surrounding country has but this one stench. It was too wet to camp out, which we would have to do in our cart owing to the loss of our tent. Seven days we endured this wretched place, expecting at any hour to be prostrated with enteric fever. Fortunately this was not to be. The way in which we entered the town was unique if not agreeable. Following our guide, the road seemed good ; whipping up our horses we proceeded a little faster, soon, however, to find ourselves propelled through the air and standing on our heads in the road. My companion went first with a shout and a curse, while I followed. The horses were high up on the sidewalk, quietly waiting our pleasure. The cart remained upright, intact, and we were not hurt, and so we sat in the dust for a while to collect our wits, notebooks, and other things. Meanwhile my new assistant was raving at things in general, especially at our guide and his own sciatica, interwoven with peals of laughter. We were in good humour to think we had got into Ladysmith at last in spite of all our troubles, and on the first day, following close up behind General

Buller, one of the two first civilians allowed through the lines.

March 2nd.—General Buller made an unofficial entrance into the town from the opposite side, the people all having congregated at the Iron Bridge entrance. To-morrow we are promised a fête, and with what strength is left among the people they

GORDON HIGHLANDERS IN LADYSMITH.

endeavour to make some preparation. Meanwhile we go on a snap-shotting expedition; first to the Gordon Highlanders, from whom I received a warm welcome, having known many of them at Aldershot. It is wonderful how they lived during all these terrible months under constant fire. Under the guidance of Colonel Scott, commanding the Gordons, who spent much time in showing me how they lived in huge excavations, down which they went as soon as the warning-bugle would sound—one man being always on duty with his telescope, watching the enemy's movements to give warning when he saw Long Tom trained on the camp. We then visited the spot where Colonel Conyngham lost his life, only a few steps from the camp. The Gordon boys, who loved their leader well, had erected a stone pyramid in his honour, on which is inscribed :

" On this spot Colonel W. H. Conyngham, V.C., commanding the Gordon Highlanders, was mortally wounded on January 6, 1900."

Just beyond the camp the deep river-bed gave our men considerable shelter and the free use of the water to bathe in, and in spite of the hardships all looked well and hearty—which comes of having a grand foundation to build upon, a clean life through and through.

The transport waggons have not reached us yet, and there is no food for horse or man. Some sweet biscuits and a drink from my water-bottle I had to call my breakfast, and then go in search of horse-food, having to employ Kaffirs to cut grass and bring it in in sacks. From early morning the roads are crowded with transport waggons, and everybody reads " food," and already thinks how good it will taste, poor souls. One and a quarter biscuits is a day's rations, and hardly any wood to cook anything with.

March 3rd.—Becomes a busy day for all. By 10 a.m. we have secured a Biograph and other pictures of the beleaguered Gordon Highlanders *en route* from the camp to welcome the entrance of the

GENERAL WHITE WELCOMING THE RELIEVING FORCE.

relief column, headed by General Buller and Staff. This is our next picture, but regretfully we must face the sun to secure it.   Every facility has been given us by Colonel Scott, in command of the High-landers, who, with other regiments, line the streets on both sides—our cart being conspicuously a nuisance, from the back of which we took the Bios.   The cart had to displace the soldiers, the back reaching out into the street as we had no tripod ; this we had found impossible to drag over the mountain, and so had left it behind.

It was a gala day.   Soon every one was cheering as the cavalcade approached : Sir Redvers Buller followed by his Staff, then troop after troop, cavalry, artillery, and our own naval guns, all welcomed vociferously and with much shaking of hands as the men dashed up to greet some old friends.

Several snaps taken that day show this as well as many other scenes of interest.   Meanwhile General White and Staff remained quietly on horseback, saluting every now and then as our relief column passed.   They all laughed heartily as a soldier was seen riding with a chicken attached to his saddle just here.   Many in the crowd who had life left to talk were saying that they never had despaired of our coming, only the disappointment was bitter each time they had heard of our set-backs.   There was much amusement while waiting for Sir Redvers and the relief forces, when a huge waggon hove in sight, solemnly passing down through our ranks laden with dead horses, now happily no longer needed for food.   I found standing at my side Winston Churchill.   When all had passed, parchments were brought out highly illuminated, on which the welcome address was inscribed. General Buller and General White, each the recipient, one from the other. Then followed up as quickly as possible the big naval 4.7 guns, which were unfortunately somewhat late in making entrance owing to the oxen giving out. And so the day closed with great joy and peace in the hearts of these poor, half-dead, released prisoners.

On my return to our odoriferous abode I discovered that my experiment to save the life of a wretched horse had failed (as I fear), for the brute is on its side and so weak it can hardly lift its head. Pity it should die just when there seems to be a promise of plenty. A snap-shot of its mate I secured while out to-day, a fair sample of how the poor beasts looked, all skin and bone.

The town has escaped miraculously, I think, considering the thousands of shells that have been thrown into it. Over three hundred shots were made before they succeeded in striking the town hall.

March 4th.—As nothing is to happen for a day or so, I decided to risk the intense heat and try to reach Umblewana's lofty heights in company with one of the officers of the *Terrible*. At ten we depart with a few biscuits and one water-bottle. We press our horses well forward over the grassy plain until we reach the once Boer country homes, or holes in the ground, and scrambling up over and through endless ditches, dongas, &c., we commence our ascent over huge boulders, the road becoming more and more precipitous. What a time these fellows must have had getting to the top. They must have gone that way, as I followed their spoor.

Mr. Winston Churchill.

THE RELIEVING FORCE PASSING THROUGH LADYSMITH.

Finally it became too steep to ride, for fear of tipping backwards. After several rests we reached tableland and an appalling stench ; the very horses snorting for fresh air. Quickly we pushed through the Boer camps, holding our noses in sheer self-defence, disturbing, as we went, huge carrion birds from their revolting feast.

We visited the spot where once Long Tom

FAIR SAMPLE OF HOW THE HORSES LOOKED IN LADYSMITH.

reposed trying to destroy our people, and from which he had to make a sudden exit, and also the abandoned searchlight electric station. It seemed a pity to see a new Siemens and Halske dynamo left to weather it, as well as a good English boiler and other appurtenances. The searchlight lamp itself was gone. We lunched later on, when far away from the Boer camp though, in the exact spot where the telegraph office or tent had been. Could the little battery that 1 then held in my hand only speak and divulge all the messages it had helped to transmit, it would, I felt, be deeply interesting. The wires are still up, and reach from this spot far out and over the hills towards Boerland. This can only remain for a very short while Boerland, as General Warren and others are now chasing them on and up over the border. A snap I made from this height shows the town and valley far down below us, surrounded by the everlasting hills.

If I could only disassociate Ladysmith and its surroundings from dead things, I think I could enjoy it all the more. Our return trip took very much longer, as we wished to see how the Boers lived in those holes in the ground, curiously enough expecting, as they did, to remain there and frighten us away. There were tables, chairs, benches, beds, and even pictures hanging on the earth walls, and bits of looking-glass stuck into them. It is known that their wives and children were often found with them, and many of them shot. One poor woman said as she was dying, "My husband told me I must come, and I came, and now I am dying. There are many of us poor women dragged to the front thus." She wore a bandolier and carried a carbine, and was shot through both breasts.

Our jaded beasts brought us back to town before dark, very thankful to get to bed and oblivion ; this was denied me, however. My new assistant, who had remained behind, had become very much worse, and in the night shouted in a stentorian voice all kinds of incomprehensible things, waking the neighbours and giving me food for a good laugh. He said it was a nightmare. I have been writing all

ON TOP OF UMBLEWANA,
WHERE ONCE "LONG TOM" REPOSED.

night to try and catch up, as the mail leaves in a few hours, and it is now nearly light, morning, so I must stop and continue Ladysmith doings for next mail.

(LADYSMITH CONTINUED.)

Durban, April, 1900.—Written in bed. I was forced regretfully to suspend the record of my experiences at Ladysmith, owing to a sudden attack of enteric fever, which obliged me temporarily to retire from public life. The pestilential town where I was forced to remain seven days was kind enough to present me not with its freedom, but with some of the already too fashionable enteric microbe. The disease postponed its development until I had returned to Durban and had packed ready to return to Capetown, at which place I expected to pick up my new camera; General Miles, Chief of Staff, having already provided me with several valuable letters.

The enteric specialist in attendance at this hospital says that I have the mildest case he has ever known. I had the " deadly spots " and the fever. Both have now disappeared, and while my guardian angels are watching for a relapse, I am enjoying myself with a chat on paper as I want to complete the record of my doings at Ladysmith.

The two Durban photographers who had been through the campaign refused to even enter the city, preferring not to risk their lives, so they returned empty-handed. I remained a week, and, as usual, escaped miraculously. Let me give a few specific dates and recollections.

Ladysmith, March 5th–8th.—Terrifically hot.

The town is rendered almost unendurable with the stenches. The coolie stretcher-bearers are to be seen everywhere. It is always easy to tell the dead from the sick even at a distance. In the case of a death the stretchers are closed up tight, whereas if it is merely a case of illness they are left partially open. I was much struck with the cat-like glide of the four coolies as they slid rapidly along on their bare feet.

While gazing at these dismal *cortèges*, I became aware of a sound so joyous and triumphant that instinctively I put spurs to my horse and soon galloped into sight of the Gordon Highlanders, who were playing " The Cock of the North " for all they were worth, as they accompanied the *Powerful* men, their companions of the siege, to the train. There was wild enthusiasm—and no wonder, for their work was done and well done, and all were happy.

We soon reached the station, where the procession was met by our Naval Brigade relief column (that to which I had been attached). After much hand-shaking, the Gordon pipers formed in a ring and played some wild, inspiring airs while the men entered the train. We lingered to catch the last glimpse of them as they hung from the windows waving their straw hats and shouting their adieux to the crowd which had availed itself of every available spot on the platform. The part played by this Naval Brigade with their 4.7 guns can hardly be over-estimated. During all these long months they had been success-ful in keeping the enemy at a respectful distance, and often covered General White's sorties with their fire. In spite of the fearful hardships they had undergone, they looked, I thought, remarkably well as they strode along in their nautical blues, having discarded their khakis that day.

To-day we taste bread again. What a treat! We had jam too. Commander Limpus honoured us with his good company, and when we wound up with a little whisky and rainwater, we felt there was nothing to complain of. After saying goodbye, I wandered through the town to see if I had missed anything. It was still inert; dead as a door-nail; almost every shop closed, and nothing going on except the endless bullock transports coming in with food and fire-wood, besides a large number of waggons containing champagne and whisky. Rows of people were standing waiting for their rations to be doled out at the back of the city hall. Many were wretchedly emaciated, others surprisingly well preserved. Everywhere I saw palpable evidences of the enemy's work, notably, huge holes through house-tops and walls. Whenever I stopped my horse for a moment to examine these effects of the bombardment, I was surrounded by the town-folk, anxious to tell me of their hairbreadth escapes as the shells passed through the rooms, narrowly missing the occupants. In one instance a huge piece of shell just missed the town clerk's head by an inch or two, as he rose from his desk, burying itself in the wall beyond. I was shown the spot. I collected several mementos of this and other such experiences and sent them to London.

The town-hall was the enemy's pet target, at which, it is stated, they fired between three and four hundred shots before doing any material damage. Even then they only carried away half the turret, as will be seen from the snap-shot.

As I required certain items of information, I paid a visit to the staff officers' quarters, which were located in a convent on a hill; after which I made tracks for my own diggings, which were loathsome, though no worse, I believe, than those situated in other parts of the town.

That night was a record night, made hideous by the most unearthly caterwauling caused by a dispute over a choice bit of dead cow. To this concert my companion contributed liberally. When not shouting or growling in his sleep, he promenaded up and down the verandah, cursing everything and everybody, including the day he was born. I soon discovered he had lighted his pipe (this at 2 a.m.) and was smoking furiously, quite oblivious to the fact that I was receiving the full benefit of the filthy Boer weed. My olfactories had a picnic that night—a choice of delightful odours, dead horse and bullock, carbolic, Boer tobacco, &c.

March 8th.—General White left the town to-day, and again the Gordon Highlanders were there to see him off. He looked very pale and feeble as he made his farewell speech to his soldiers, who met him with the greatest enthusiasm. Several shouted " Goodbye, and God bless you," as he disappeared into the station.

It was a very affecting sight to watch the tender solicitude of his officers, one and all, as they crowded around him, wishing him a speedy recovery. As the train moved out slowly from the overcrowded station, cheer after cheer rent the air.

An hour later we were off, too, in our Cape cart, only too delighted to shake the dust and microbes from off our clothes.

By this time the Colenso bridge had been repaired, so that we were able to take the main road back, which was a great comfort. It was a very long trek, without much excitement, except that afforded by the stallions, who had a refreshing shindy in harness, biting and tearing at each other, and finally smashing in the footboard, while I occupied myself in thrashing them apart. I am quite sure I have run just as much risk with these splendid devils as I have from the enemy's shell ; nevertheless I forgive them, in view of their unexcelled speed and power of endurance. On one occasion I remember turning a kopje, or corner of a hillside, and finding that I was in the direct line of fire, it took me just five seconds to veer the horses round and tear back. I was not biographically engaged that day, and saw no reason for exposing myself. What a race that was ! It reminded me exactly of my Russian troika experiences, when my wife and I with two friends had bribed our driver to catch the then incoming train at the station for St. Petersburg on our return from Peterhoff, where we had been visiting Rubinstein.

I had never thought to pass over the dread Boer entrenchments overlooking Colenso, but towards evening, as we reached the last hill-top and commenced our descent towards Colenso river, we had a splendid view of them. It was a sight to see the thousands of stone barricades and fortifications all along the roads and hillsides and far out into the plain, to the very water's edge. It was from these places that they fired upon our people and killed so many at the battle of Colenso.

Winding our way gradually down the mountainside we soon reached the bridge, which had been temporarily repaired to allow the traffic to take its course. One of our chief gunners, Bates by name, of the 4.7 Naval Brigade, threw down the middle of the bridge after the third shot, to prevent the Boers from bringing over their guns. This is considered a marvellous shot, being at a range of over five miles. That night it rained in torrents. I found myself obliged to leave my man with horses and Cape cart to await a favourable day and hour for securing railroad transport, a difficult task as our troops were swarming every hour into the station on their way to join Lord Roberts. They were all, later on, recalled before they could sail, however.

These notes cover my experience from Southampton, October 14, 1899, to the end of the first week in March, 1900. They are of necessity abrupt and incomplete jottings, as the conditions were not favourable to continuity of thought.

Durban, April 7th.—While lying here in the sanatorium, enjoying the ministrations of the white doves of peace, after the dogs of war, I amuse myself in writing my belated diary, and awaiting the portable camera which is to serve me in the coming campaign with Lord Roberts. It may be that before joining Lord Roberts I will get one or two views at the point which General Buller has now reached, and then back here to Durban to catch the first boat for Capetown, thence rail up to Lord Roberts' position.

April 19, 1900. On board.—On April 16th we left Durban for Capetown, with Cape cart, horses, and all our baggage, hoping to be able to reach Pretoria by joining General Roberts' column ; many of our friends coming to the pier to see us off, with sacks of fruit and other useful presents. As soon as we were hoisted on board the *Dunottar Castle* in the basket, Captain Rigby and officers greeted us most cordially, and many questions were asked on both sides.

The trip was more or less uneventful until we reached East London, where we were told we must remain for three days, on which information I decided to land and take train inland to one of the ostrich farms, near the quaint little town of Uitenhage. Before proceeding to the farms, we spent a few hours going about to see how the sheep's wool was washed and packed for shipment, the machinery for this work being so designed as to cleverly take the place of the workmen's hands. The horticulturist of the town showed us a number of rare and (to me) unknown plants, seeds and bulbs, many of which we took with us and later sent to England.

At noon we took train part of the way back to a station called "Perseverance." How it ever got such a name remains a mystery, as there are but two houses, very far apart, one of which is owned by Mr. Hudson, where he had been over twelve years ostrich farming. He received us in a most friendly manner, inviting us in and offering us refreshments, of which we gladly partook, as the day was intensely warm.

When we had somewhat cooled off, we were shown the monkey and other household pets. Mr. Hudson's youngest child delighted in exhibiting the little brute's antics, while it studied its face in a hand mirror ; indeed, it was the most laughable thing I had ever seen.

The homestead is dreary in its barren surroundings, and I think it marvellous how these wonderful pioneers of a new country stand it. Sketches and snaps taken on the spot will almost give one the blues.

This depression was soon dispelled by a formidable squad of military-looking giant birds, which, barelegged, but otherwise well plumed—except on the neck and head—made their way towards us in a most stately manner. After some running around one was caught for plucking. Before releasing him, Mr. Hudson dared me to ride the bird, which just then required three men to hold him. I knew I must not hesitate or I should be lost. I glanced around at the soil to see how many sharp rocks there were (as I hoped to visit other climes) and I made a dive for its back, only to be sent flying. My third attempt was successful. I learned by this experience to get on its back when down, and await the awful upward plunge which speedily came. I only know that it was, without exception, one of the most absurdly wild rides I ever had, as we tacked about while I held on tightly to the wings. I didn't remain very long on my perch, and slid off behind, a trick all bicyclists have had to learn when about to crash into something hard. Meanwhile my companion had been busy snapping the show.

In our wanderings we came across several skeletons of these monster birds, which we carried back to the little station to await our train back to Port Elizabeth. No wonder that my weight was but as an additional feather on the bird's back, when you compare the size of the thigh-bone with that of a man's.

This ostrich farming, I am told, is one of the most paying businesses in the world. They take care of themselves, need no feeding, and all you have to do

COLONEL LONG.
(Photographed at Nelson Hotel, Capetown.

is to pluck, and look after the young birds occasionally. Our friend, Mr. Hudson, is a tall, portly gentleman, doesn't look as if he had had a care in the world, and delights to show off his fourteen children. I marvel often at the pluck of these early settlers.

Nothing very interesting happened *en route* to Capetown.

Capetown.—On leaving our old friend the s.s. *Dunottar Castle*, I drove to Mount Nelson Hotel, which is beautifully situated, high above the town—on the only healthy part, it is said—and was lucky in securing delightful quarters.

The cart, horses, and baggage were distributed between the stables and storerooms, and I prepared to make my rounds among the military powers. Much time was taken up writing and wiring to Bloemfontein headquarters and awaiting the replies; meanwhile, I had the pleasure of cultivating several of my acquaintances met by chance during the last six months' campaign, who had congregated at this Mount Nelson, a veritable oasis in this desert of sameness and unhealthiness.

Several of my friends submitted with grace to the kodaking process, among whom were Colonel Long, Colonel Templer, Lord Bryan Leighton, Major Jones (Natal Press Censor), &c., &c.

After a wearisome day of getting ready and interviewing, I was always grateful for those congenial' evenings quietly spent among friends, while listening to the divinely inspired "Parsifal" and other classic productions rendered by the Mount Nelson String Trio, who are finished musicians.

May 12th.—Colonel Templer, my good friend of Aldershot days, has arranged a splendid picture for the Biograph this morning, so we prepare to drive out to Greenpoint to witness the experiment of using his traction engines to drag the large 6-in. guns into position for practice.

The camera we placed on the road close to the

VIEW SEEN FROM THE BACK OF THE HON. CECIL RHODES'
PALATIAL HOME.

Boer prisoners' enclosure, were we could see the fellows in groups talking fight, I suppose, although I fancy they have had enough and would be glad to let up. I took a snap-shot of the sentinel who despatched a suspicious character who would not reply to his challenge. Of course he was a Boer.

A shout from some bystanders warned us of the arrival of the engine and gun. My instruction to them was to " go like h——," which order I discovered later had been literally transmitted, much to the amusement of the kindly officer in charge. It was a sight ! By going faster than a walk it obliged soldier and officer to run as they passed the camera, which they had to do at their utmost speed in order to keep up.

Unfortunately I wasn't able to stay to this gun practice, as I had to rush back and dress so as not to be too late for lunch at Mr. Rhodes' palatial home at Rondebush, some distance out of town.

After a sharp ride of three-quarters of an hour I came in view of the well-known avenue of giant trees, twisting and turning on its way to the white house, a welcome shelter from the sun.

Mr. Rhodes didn't keep me very long as I waited in his luxuriously equipped parlour. He had been visiting his horses, which I had the pleasure of seeing on a previous visit under the guidance of his sister, Miss Rhodes, who is passionately fond of the dumb brutes.

Meeting cordially, we went in to lunch, and thanks to Lady Edward Cecil, who sat at my side, with Mr. Rhodes on the other, I learned much regarding this earthly paradise called " Groot Schuur."

I was especially interested in the curious wild

things with which I came in contact in the course
of my wanderings through Mr. Rhodes' domains.
These seemed to have no end, encompassing mile
after mile of land, bearing up towards the great
towering Dantaic Table Mountain and Devil's
Peak.

DR. JAMESON (AFTER-DINNER SNAP).

When speaking of Rhodesia, Mr. Rhodes turned in
his chair and, pointing out through the open doors,
remarked : " If any portion of Rhodesia could compare with that, I would ask you to come ; but there's
nothing like *that*." And, indeed, I can hardly

DINING-ROOM AT GROOT SCHUUR.

believe any place could be more beautiful ; and he seems to love it. As he spoke, a deliciously cool breeze bore in on its wings the most exquisite perfume of flowers, which could be seen terraced up and up towards a rich grove of dark evergreen trees, behind and beyond which, grand old Table Mountain waits, " watching for the world to die." To cap the wonder of the scene, a few moments after the whole top of the flat table, two miles in length, became obscured by a delicate semi-transparent mist which soon settled over the edge of the rugged cliffs.

Among the guests there were Lady Charles Bentinck, Dr. Jameson (of the Jameson Raid), Mr. Rhodes, and others.

After the repast, Mr. Rhodes called me to his desk and gave me a letter to his college chum, Lord Kitchener, and to his diamond manager, asking them to please give me " every assistance." The last-mentioned instruction meant a few bags of diamonds, I suppose !

I enjoyed my visit immensely. Before leaving, Mr. Rhodes begged me not to hurry, and to roam about, which I did. After getting several views of the interior and exterior of the house, I went again up among the animals, making friends with zebras, kafirkranes, tigers, lions, &c. ; the lions were strangely tame, submitting calmly and with decided indifference to being snapped. I returned somewhat awed by the almost unparalleled accumulation of beautiful and unique accoutrements and accessories of a home so far from civilisation.

So, with a dozen letters of introduction, I pro-ceeded to Bloemfontein, leaving my assistant behind to follow with Cape cart and horses.

Friday.—At 9.30 the corridor train left Capetown, and for three days and nights we had a royal time on board. We had by good luck the first detachment of the Scottish National Red Cross Hospital Corps and nurses, together with the doctors and officers, feeding as best we could *en route* at the wretched stations at any hour; once at 12.30 midnight for supper, instead of six or seven. It was strange how little grumbling there was and how much fun. We had suffered before, so made the best of it.

The last day we should have been in at Bloemfontein at 8 p.m., but didn't arrive until the following dawn, and then only within thirteen miles of the town; and not having had much supper we were starved. At 6.30 a.m. we, on our other half of the corridor train, with heads covered up to keep out the bitter cold of the night, heard a cheery voice say, " Have a cup of tea and some biscuits ? " and there, as though in a vision, we beheld the Red Cross ladies with the tea and biscuits in their hands.

We greeted our benefactresses with cheer after cheer. Oh, were we not cold, hungry, and grateful!

At nine we reached Bloemfontein, all disembarking, as we could go no further. And here we stuck, waiting for orders from the front to proceed. Meanwhile I busied myself wiring to Kroonstadt to Lord Kitchener to help me up with the Cape cart and horses, which undertaking seems so difficult, owing to the congested state of the traffic.

I visited camp after camp, lunching here and there with the bravest of England's heroes. One camp I must mention in particular, for it cannot be passed over lightly. The nobility of England,

C. B. ELLIOTT, GENERAL MANAGER, CAPE GOVERNMENT R. R.

GENERAL KELLY-KENNY AND STAFF REVIEWED THE TROOPS, IN HONOUR
OF OUR BELOVED QUEEN.

mostly millionaires, joined our forces, each paying
£130. They are known as the 13th Regiment of
Imperial Yeomanry, commanded by Colonel B. E.
Spragge, numbering 543, among whom are the Duke
of Cambridge's Own.   Lord Longford raised his
squadron in Dublin, consisting of hunting men from
nearly every part of Ireland ; quite 90 per cent. of
these are gentlemen. I might say the same of the
46th Ulsters, raised by Captain E. Rokeley-Robinson.
All their pay goes to the Widows and Orphans Fund.
A splendid lot of fellows, not one thinking it
beneath him to take care of his horse, stables, or
whatever comes to hand.

BATTALION STAFF.

> Lieut.-Colonel B. E. Spragge, D.G.O.
> Lieut.-Colonel A. G. Holland.
> Captain and Adjutant E. Rokeley-Robinson.
> Medical Officer, Captain F. A. Hadley.
> Veterinary Officer, Lieutenant E. D. Fenner.
> Quarter-Master, Lieutenant H. Dickinson.

The last-named being my jolly and irresistibly
humorous railway companion from Capetown.
These fine fellows left to-day, and did their utmost to
persuade me to join them. Had I done so I should
have been captured. But I must wait for my Cape
cart and horses, which are following by order of
Lord Kitchener, to whom I wired ; no one paying
the slightest attention to any other orders.   Every
time I get into trouble I wire to his lordship, and
immediately get a satisfactory answer.

May 24*th.*—I must skip much, and simply touch
on things as they occur, as I seem to find less and

less time for these daily notes, which often are sadly in arrears.

General Kelly-Kenny and Staff reviewed the troops, in honour of our beloved Queen. The review took place just outside the town, " by the Willows," and I, as usual, received every attention and courtesy from the powers—all officers, friends, or strangers doing what they could to assist in making these living records of events that can never be repeated.

May 27th.—Chief of Police, Lieutenant G. D. Gray, on whom I called, gave me a letter to the gaol, for Mr. Mulligan to help me get photos of the Boers, besides handing me the following interesting and unique document :

COPY OF TRANSLATION OF WINSTON CHURCHILL'S WARRANT OF ARREST (BLOEMFONTEIN POLICE).

(*Translated from the Dutch into English by a Dutchman.*)

Description of a deserter prisoner of war named Winston Spencer Churchill, escaped out of the State Model School, Pretoria, on the 12th December, 1899.

Englishman, 25 years old, about 5 feet 8 inches high—indifferent built—walks a little with a bend forward—pale appearance—red brownish hair—small moustache hardly perceptible—talks through the nose, cannot pronounce the letter S properly, and does not know one word of Dutch.

When last seen had a brown suit of clothes.

The portrait that was taken about 18 months ago can be seen at the police-station, Bloemfontein.

The undersigned requests any one finding him, to arrest him and report to the Commissioner of Police O.V.S.

(*Signed*)

J. A. E. MARKUS.

INTERIOR OF GYMNASIUM OF THE MODEL SCHOOL,
PRETORIA, SHOWING HOW SOME OF THE PRISONERS
MADE THEIR ESCAPE.

The day was bitterly cold, and as our Cape cart, horses, and servant had just arrived by train, we hitched up, and drove out to the massive structure to exercise the poor brutes, who had been *en route* five days. I found it a tedious undertaking to persuade these fellows to submit to just what I wanted.

After nearly an hour's talk in German I persuaded first one and then another to join in. I expected every minute to get my throat cut while sitting in the rotunda inside the prison, with over thirty of them crowding around me, some fine-looking fellows, but some regular cut-throats, terrible in their rage at being caged up.

I felt that if I could persuade the worst types I should win the day, and so concentrated my whole attention and energy in their direction, getting them all in good humour by stories and persuasions, strictly avoiding the war as a topic. Soon I succeeded in getting them to ask for pictures. Here was my keynote. I grouped them outside in eights and twelves, and snapped them, and finally got twenty to pass the Biograph in review. It was a rather exhausting process. As time won't allow me to describe more fully this (to me) most remarkable experience, I must proceed to the Annexation Ceremony, of which I was quietly told by a private message from the Provost Marshal, who asked me to prepare for the event and to use the balcony of the Military Club House if I wished.

May 28*th*.—We were up early ; before breakfast had unloaded our Cape cart at the Club entrance, and soon had the machine set up in the very best of positions, overlooking the large market-square, in the centre of which a flag-pole had been erected secretly the night before, so that no one knew about it. In fact, the great Anti-Imperialistic Society had given out that they would hold a mass meeting on June 4th to discuss the question of holding all these states free and under self-rule. It must have been a veritable bomb exploding among them to see the flag-staff and hear the news. There has been much laughter at their expense.

I received a message from headquarters that I must be ready by 11 a.m. for the coming of the troops, and soon we could hear bands playing in every direction as they marched into the square from the various camps surrounding the town, as they poured into the square manœuvring into position, as they ranged themselves around the flag, leaving a large open space for the dignitaries, officers, &c., to come. At noon Governor-General Prettyman and Staff, preceded by a mounted escort, approached the flag-staff, and as soon as the proclamation had been read in a loud, clear voice by that gentleman, Her Majesty's name for the new colony given, the flag was unfurled, cheer after cheer rending the air, while the troops presented arms.

And so we have another good slice of mother earth in the Orange Valley River Colony added to our long list of possessions. Long live the Queen! It was a glorious event. Thanks to the Biograph, which faithfully recorded this magnificent scene, the people of the world who were not as fortunate as those present will see what it saw, and doubtless sing " God save the Queen."

Kroonstadt, May 29th.—Have left Bloemfontein at last, after wiring repeatedly to Lord Kitchener to

BOER PRISONERS AT BLOEMFONTEIN.

15

ANNEXATION CEREMONY AT BLOEMFONTEIN, MAY 28, 1900.

get me up the line towards Pretoria, with no result.
This was not the fault of Lord Kitchener, who sent
three telegrams to the authorities to the effect that
I be given railroad facilities for Cape cart and horses;
personal passes I had received some weeks before.
They claimed that they needed the trucks to send
up food for the soldiers, but having proved that each
day there were several in excess of what was needed
for this purpose, I can only say that the assistant
transport agent acted against Lord Kitchener's
orders and caused me endless worry and serious
delay, and nearly wrecked my highest ambition,
namely, to get to Pretoria in time for the entrance
of the troops. I interviewed every one from the
Governor-General to the brakesman of the trucks,
and finally succeeded in engaging and paying for
two trucks. We were shunted on to the 11.30, our
Cape cart and ourselves in one, the horses in the
other.

Just as the train was about to move off three
officers were found without accommodation, whom
of course I invited to join us in our flat car, and it
is with much pleasure that I look back to that unique
trip. Fortunately (thanks to my ever thoughtful
assistant, Mr. Cox, who had commandeered a huge
tarpaulin) we were sheltered from the bitter night
cold and scorching sun during the day ; and what
with a good supply of roast chicken and fresh bread
which the Bloemfontein Hotel had put up for me,
we had a jolly supper interlarded with the narration
of thrilling experiences of the campaign.

Unfortunately our friends had to leave us at
Wynburg Junction, at nine or ten that night, while
we jolted along on our not too soft beds or springless

cattle-truck. We slept, however. At each stop, of
which there were many, the only sound would be
the stamping of our horses in the next truck, or the
ramp of a train guard.

Had there been any fear of a surprise we were
well guarded, having over fifteen hundred men with
us, piled in and out of every truck. We were
obliged to go on with extreme caution, for fear of
pitfalls, and gladly welcomed the dawn of another
day.

May 30*th.*—We arrived at Kroonstadt at 4 a.m.,
and after setting our food on the Mutograph (which
throughout the trip we used for a table) we break-
fasted; and, learning that the train would take a
rest for several hours, and perhaps not leave before
one o'clock, we proceeded to " do " the wretched
place, which is large but painfully plain—a vast
expanse of galvanised sheet-iron covered buildings,
barely boasting of a one-story structure. We passed
a chemist's and a large hotel now converted into a
hospital. In fact almost every large building,
including the big church, we found packed with
sufferers, attended by our brave Red Cross nurses,
painfully overworked, untiring in their endeavours
to alleviate their sufferings. The court-house, with
its crowd of warriors giving up their arms, arrested
our attention, and we watched them as they handed
in their weapons, wearing a sullen, dogged look on
their faces, which they tried to hide as they were
snapped.

After a later breakfast at the Central Hotel, the
one and only place we could find, we continued our
wanderings among the defences, river banks, &c.,
meeting groups, every now and then, of harmless (?),

THE CHURCH AT KROONSTADT.

FREE STATERS WAITING TO SURRENDER.

fully armed Free Staters on their way to the court-house to swear in their allegiance.

Finding little else of interest, we pushed on with the body of troops for safe escort, as there was every fear of an attack ; and although we escaped, others who followed in our wake were fired on, and several were wounded.   I felt at the time that it was owing to our large body of men that we were left alone.

Another long day and night on the cattle-truck, then next evening at 5 p.m. we were all dumped on the veldt, and those who were unfortunate enough to be without horses and Cape cart were in a sore plight.   The train crept on seven miles further to railhead, beyond which everything was blown up as far as the Vaal River.

Later on I discovered why we had been put off so unceremoniously.   It was owing to the fact that there were no means of unloading the horses or cart at railhead.

At six the same evening we were off and packed; my servant, remaining on the truck with the heavy things, went on to railhead, seven miles ahead.

It soon got dark, and, stumbling along for a few miles, we were compelled to pitch tent before attempting to cross Rhenoster River that night. The nearest tent we found was occupied by two kind-hearted Scotchmen, who immediately came over to us and helped put up the tent, light a fire, &c.   They were stationed here superintending the repair of the line, and to put up·water-tanks, which had been blown down by the Boers.

The cold was intense, so as soon as we had finished supper and tied up the horses for the night we pulled on our knitted nightcaps, sent us by a kind friend, and, crawling into our bags, tried to sleep. This last we found a hopeless task, as our horses, half-starved that day, proved troublesome. One had broken away, and the other was neighing loudly for his friend, otherwise I should never have known of the occurrence until it was too late. Clever beast! We never got warm again, and, shivering, we rose at dawn and ran a race to get our blood up. Oh, how we welcomed the sun's warm rays! I do not blame the sun-worshippers for making such a fuss over their god, if they have such cold nights to endure.

May 31*st.*—Early we get away, and descend the precipitous banks of the Rhenoster River, ford the stream, and scramble up the other side and away, not without getting some good pictures of the terrible effect of dynamite on the railroad bridge, where huge iron girders may be seen twisted entirely out of shape as they rest against the great stone columns now in ruins.

The Boers seem to have done far more damage to the Free State railways than to their own.

We soon reach the railhead, the train having gone across the river on a temporary structure, and, finding our servant and camera paraphernalia, we pushed on, occasionally stopping at some desolate-looking farm to beg for bread. How glad we were to get a stale loaf—which, however, I only succeeded in getting by much blarney in German.

At 2 p.m. we were all done up, and outspanned at a certain William Melville's farm, called Prospect, at Vredeford Road, where the good Scotch wife made us a cup of tea, while we brought in our

MODDER RIVER, O.R.C.

RAILROAD CULVERT BLOWN UP BY THE BOERS NEAR THE RHENOSTER
RIVER.

lunch.   We took this occasion to listen to narrations
of marvellous deeds of heroism and loyalty to our
cause on their part and that of their thirteen- and
eleven-year old boys, who had succeeded in robbing
the Boers of their dynamite, which the latter had
placed in and about several culverts and railroad
bridges.   The little chaps, whom we of course
photographed, had for some hours been watching
the Boers creeping silently about preparing things
to their satisfaction, and as soon as they left for
a while the boys stole down at dark.   Together
they and their Kaffir boy, John Ramanana, stole
the lot, going from bridge to culvert backwards and
forwards to the farm, bringing it to their father who
buried it.   At dawn the Boers returned ; the train
passed, but there was no explosion as they had
evidently expected there should be.

On my arrival at Pretoria I made a full report
of this to the Provost Marshal, and I hope the boys
may be suitably rewarded.   However this may be,
I bought a good veldt pony from them to help me
along the remainder of the road to Pretoria.   Otherwise I doubt if we should ever have reached that
long-sought-for place ; for we found hundreds of
oxen and horses by the roadside dead and dying,
having dropped down from sheer exhaustion, utterly
unable to pull through the miles and miles of deep,
heavy sand.   The horror of this scene is something
I shall not easily forget.   We had to stop and rest
every hundred yards or so, as the wheels continually
sank deep down in a hopelessly stick-fast way.
Although our thoroughbreds were game all through,
and were straining every nerve, assisted by the little
pony we had hitched in front, on which one of us

rode, it was impossible for us to make more than
a mile an hour. This was rather discouraging, in
view of the fact that previously our usual average
had been from twenty-six to twenty-eight miles
a day. That night we camped in the open again,
as far off the beaten track as possible, so as to avoid
the deadly stench that arose from the carrion, always
worse at night.

We had found a small spot of ground unburnt
by the Boers, on which we let our beasts loose to
graze, finding that they stuck to the grass, avoiding
the black, grim veldt beyond and all around them.
Soon we had our tent up, fire lit, and were enjoying
a good supper—or so it tasted after our fatigue of
the day. Then we slept soundly, until wakened
in the early hours by the bitter cold. This was
June 2nd. We were up, packed, &c., by daylight,
and did thirty-five miles—a severe strain on the
horses with such a load ; and at night, after this
day of incessant hard work and long marches, we
reached a distant farm, situated on a high kopje. It
being quite dark when we arrived, we got badly
entangled in barbed wire, and were afflicted besides
with evil smells and with a sense of insecurity by
not knowing how many, if any, Boers might be
lurking among the trees. Leaving the servant with
the horses I pushed on, creeping up to the walls,
listening at every few steps ; when among the bushes
I heard the branches being pushed aside, and, picking
up courage, I advanced to a shadowy form. This
I hailed, but receiving no answer I followed hard
upon the retreating figure over rocks and cactus
right up to the house, my companion at this point
catching up with me just in time to witness my

THE LITTLE CHAPS WHO SAVED THE BRIDGE.

VAAL RIVER BRIDGE—EFFECTS OF DYNAMITE.

discomfiture and relief, at discovering only a lonely cow.

We had to know our surroundings and neighbours, of course, always before camping. We outspanned, in spite of possible danger, lit our fire, and trusted to Providence. After supper we wandered about in the dark to find water for the horses, and were well repaid by discovering a little pond, from which a stream was flowing, showing it wasn't stagnant.

After rather a restless night we arose nearly frozen, as usual, and moved on as quickly as possible to encounter the most terrible roads in all my experience, better call them no roads at all. Our beasts were covered with lather, and were almost losing their breath, when to aid them we had to push behind, or all of us tug at a wheel, the while lashing our patient and willing horses into continued great effort. At ten we met an officer who told us he did not think we could go any further unless we spanned a team of oxen. We, however, reached the Vaal that afternoon at two, without losing heart or a horse.

About a mile from the river we stopped half an hour to rest our horses. Here we discovered the kindest of hosts in *mein Herr Baum*, a Russian Jew, proprietor of the only store in this mining district. He did his best to fill us up with whisky from his scant supply, noticing how exhausted we were. We got a loaf and trekked on to the river, ploughing our way through deep sand. Our horses on seeing the water fairly tugged at their traces, and before long we were in heaven for a while, as we camped at the bottom of the embankment, outspanning at the water's edge. What Elysium ! What a delight-

ful bath!—but ugh! how cold. We selected our
camp spot up the stream beyond the dead horses
and bullocks ; one of these which looked particularly
fresh as it lay on its side just out of reach of the
water I touched with my foot. The wretched beast
opened its eyes and gazed intently at me with the
most pitiable expression of anguish. I had to turn
away and forget the sight. On again then, a long
pull and a pull all together, we reached the top of
the bank. Now in the Transvaal, we drove to the
railroad station, about two miles distant, through
another mining town, dreary and indescribably
lonely. I stated my case to the kindly staff officer,
who promised me a lift on the train next morning.
We slept at the station, commandeering the telegraph office for ourselves, while we put up the
horses in a room near by. At about eleven the
staff officer, with courteous and profuse apologies
for disturbing us, said, as there was not a room
better suited for his purpose he feared he must use
our telegraph office, or bedroom, for the safe-keeping
of some three hundred Boer prisoners who were
coming in on the midnight train, offering us at the
same time his quarters, which he begged we would
share with him. We got up, of course, and commenced packing, but hadn't proceeded far before he
returned and said it was all right to stay where we
were, and if the prisoners came he would try and
find other quarters for them, or keep them on the
train.

That was a night! Next door to us there were
several enteric patients, who coughed and groaned
all night. My assistant spent quite a long time in
pasting up broken windows with paper to keep out

BOER PRISONERS.

TOMMY ATKINS FINDS RED MUD A GOOD SUBSTITUTE FOR KHAKI PAINT.

the wind and cold from them. The cold towards morning was so bitter, and the wind so penetrating, that I crawled inside a cupboard and *slept*, while my feet stuck outside and froze. Later on a good cup of coffee did wonders to make me forget it all.

June 4th.—No train made up yet; prisoners just in from the front; awful-looking chaps. We had busied ourselves the night before in getting our Cape cart on to a flat car and fastened down to secure the promised lift which, alas, did not take place until late in the morning. It took us through to Elansfontein, and there we stuck with a horrible fear lest we should fail to follow in to Pretoria in time for the entry of the troops, news having just come that Lord Roberts had already pushed on. This failure, in the face of our bitter experiences, would be more than I could bear, therefore at noon we hastened to get away and reached the railroad, which was only about fifteen miles from Pretoria. We whipped up violently all the way, two men inside the cart, and my servant *à la postillon* on the little horse. We followed in after Lord Roberts, biographing him and his Staff on the outskirts of the town, and later on the flag from a fine position in the window.

Had the raising of the flag been done in the middle of the Square, then the surrounding crowd as well as the flag could have been photographed; but as it was raised several hundred feet high on the peak of the Rathhouse, the unfurling of the flag alone is shown on the Biograph.

Thus was the principal aim of our enterprise accomplished, and the heart of the Biographer was at rest.

Pretoria, June 6th.—Lord Roberts kindly consented to being biographed at headquarters with his Staff, laughingly allowing me to carry off his table with the South African map into the hot sun, whither he proceeded, followed by the Staff to discuss matters. The Biograph shows the guards saluting as he descends from the house which serves as headquarters. In the course of his progress despatches are handed to him. The background shows the flag waving. Those present were :—

Lord Lovel Roberts.

General Sir W. Nicholson, Director of Transport.

Colonel N. Chamberlain, Private Secretary.

Colonel H. Cowan, Military Secretary.

Colonel Ward, Director of Supplies.

Major Furse Daag.

Captain Waterfield.

Captain Lord Settrington, A.D.C.

Captain Lord Herbert Scott, A.A.A.

Lieutenant Earl of Kerry, A.D.C.

Lieutenant Duke of Westminster, A.D.C.

Major Edwards, I.M.S.

Colonel Sir Henry Rawlinson, D.A.A.G.

Lord Stanley, Press Censor.

Captain Stirling, Coldstream Guards.

Lieutenant Massey, Coldstream Guards.

General Sir J. Hills Johnes (personal friend of Lord Roberts ; got their V.C.s together).

Major Laing, Commander Body Guard.

The picture is known as " First Day in Pretoria at Headquarters."

Pretoria, June 7, 1900.—All is moderately quiet again after the excitement of the coming in, although several regiments are busy getting settled. The

THE MODEL SCHOOL, PRETORIA, NOW AN HOSPITAL FOR BRITISH SOLDIERS,
RECENTLY THE PRISON OF OUR OFFICERS.

RAISING THE FLAG AT PRETORIA.

17

Boers are encrusting the public buildings, giving up their arms with not too pleasant an expression on their faces. Every few minutes three or four men will ride up, armed with carbines, wearing across their broad chests their bandoliers; they dismount from their hardy little Basuto ponies to await their turn for the interview with the Provost Marshal.

All the hotels and public buildings are guarded. It is a wonderful sight to note our people making a rush for the tables at lunch and dinner time in the well-appointed Transvaal Hotel, which is under the courteous management of Mr. Hoops, who, in spite of the overwhelming crowds, never seems ruffled, but is doing his best to satisfy all. The sentries at the door have a lively time keeping out spies and suspicious characters, and it is often necessary to call upon the manager to identify this or that one. Food is at famine prices, eggs five shillings a dozen, no oatmeal, rancid butter, and very little bread; but we grin and bear it, and try to forget these little troubles in remembering that we at last occupy Pretoria. We delight in wandering about, drinking in its champagne air, and feasting our eyes on its beautiful environment. The city is almost entirely surrounded by hills, many of which are well fortified. That we got in without a blow is most fortunate, for it would have been a serious thing if this fine city had been shelled by us. During the next few days we busied ourselves driving around to get news. Botha is not far off, and we expect daily some trouble. The wires are cut and we are isolated, buried.

June 9th to 12th.—Hearing of a possible fight

within ten or twelve miles east of Pretoria we got
off at 6 a.m., soon catching up with Lord Roberts
and Staff, who were already breakfasting by the roadside with the Indian servitors in attendance ; most
picturesque sight ! Meanwhile, awaiting a move on
the part of Lord Roberts, we fed our beasts and
munched some dry biscuits ourselves. At 8.30 the
cavalcade moved on, and we followed to a stone
kopje, from which telescopic observations were made,
and heliograph messages sent to neighbouring hills.
Here we remained for an hour listening to the
distant firing before us. This was far too tanta-
lising. As soon as Lord Roberts pushed on over
the veldt, bearing to the right to join General
Pole-Carew and the naval guns, we kept to the
road, reaching the top of the hill or highest part of
the road, and from thence looked longingly down at
the valley below, and wondered if we dared proceed,
as the rifles were cracking from the surrounding
hills across the river. How I did bless (?) those
white horses and that conspicuous Cape cart, and
had I had a pot of khaki paint I think I should have
painted the beasts. It was, however, too trying not
to advance any further, and so, trusting to luck, we
drove a mile and a half further on, reaching the
celebrated Eli Marks' property at the riverside
called Vremigen. We stopped at the little inn,
Hazeldean, and found a patrol among the trees
commandeering food for their horses. I soon made
friends with the proprietor, a Russian Jew, who
gave me free access to his house, and there we
stuck for three days watching the battle by day,
not caring to proceed further than a kopje over
the river, where shrapnel was every now and then

LORD ROBERTS AND STAFF—FIRST DAY IN PRETORIA AT HEADQUARTERS.

COLONEL WARD AND LORD RAWLINSON.

bursting, though without doing much harm. Although our forces were well to the right, we lost several of our best officers, five or six in number, and twenty-five men.

Meanwhile Dr. Sholtz had received permission from Lord Roberts to try and induce Botha to see that further warfare was futile. In order to cross the enemy's lines an old-fashioned stage-coach was brought into requisition from Pretoria. Into this stepped the following : Dr. William C. Sholtz, of Capetown, British sympathiser ; J. S. Smit, Chief Commissioner of R.R. Transport, Boer ; J. F. Debeer, Chief Inspector of Officers, Boer, and the coachman, who was also a Dutch settler. They had a large white flag waving from the coach, and thus they braved the shells.

The next day, June 13th, while I was waiting with the Biograph at the river crossing for Lord Roberts, the coach returned, and I loaned Dr. Sholtz one of my greys to ride over to Lord Roberts to report the progress of these peace negotiations. We secured, before leaving, several views of coach and occupants. An hour later Dr. Sholtz returned, saying that Lord Roberts would shortly follow, and in compliance with Lord Roberts' request he would wait until his arrival. Meanwhile the coach and Boer gentlemen returned to Pretoria. As soon as our Chief and Staff made their appearance I received a message requesting the loan of my Cape cart for another run over the line. With this request I cheerfully complied. As I drove the cart up to Lord Roberts, he thanked me in his usual courtly manner. Soon Dr. Sholtz and the assistant military secretary, Captain Waterfield, were off with a rush.

This was a good opportunity, which I utilised, to
ask Lord Roberts' assistance in procuring the living
portraits of himself and Staff. He responded most
kindly to my request, saying " Certainly, certainly."
Then calling Sir Henry Rawlinson to his side he told
him what I wanted, and asked him to assist me in
making all arrangements. Sir H. Rawlinson I also
found, to my relief, most helpful and kind ; he made
an appointment with me for the day following the
morrow to plan out things. The last evening at
Hazeldean I spent with the millionaire, Eli Marks,
who told me rare stories as I sat with him on the
porch of his palatial home, where he had entertained
Kruger, Steyn, Botha, &c., &c., and above all, Lord
Roberts. He told me that Kruger was a " dear old
man," and wretchedly misguided by his ill-advisers,
that Dr. Leyds was at the bottom of all the trouble ;
and as he narrated the ups and downs of the war, he
almost cursed the last-mentioned individual, saying,
" Put all I say in your despatches, print it, publish
it to the world, for so Eli Marks says it, and means
all he says."

This Marks was practically the Transvaal Government. He seemed to hold the reins. Only a few
years ago he was peddling shoestrings, and now he
owns huge tracts of land, mines, coal, gold and
diamond, whisky distilleries, glass manufactories,
&c., &c.

June 14th and *15th.*—My Cape cart with white
flag made its appearance early this morning, and we
hastened out to greet the peace commissioners, who
do not seem to be very hopeful of good results,
although Botha received them courteously. Firing
recommences. I visited the big naval guns to watch

ARRIVAL OF DESPATCH RIDER, CAPT. SOMERS, AT HEADQUARTERS.

LORD ROBERTS AND HIS CHIEF-OF-STAFF, COLONEL SIR HENRY
RAWLINSON, D.A.A.G.

the firing, at the same time renewing my acquaintance with General Pole-Carew, whom I knew on board the *Dunottar Castle*. I reminded him of our experiences at Madeira, when he boldly pushed a rude native or Portuguese into the water, and then the row which ensued, over which we had a good laugh.

I could clearly see our men ranged along the kopje base as the enemy returned their shots, while our guns tried to clear the adjacent hills of their obnoxious presence.

After scouring the country for a few hours we paid our bill at Hazeldean, for the use of a room and for chicken stew which the Tommies stole from the kitchen during the night, then trekked back to Pretoria in order to arrange for Lord Roberts' promised series of pictures. When uncertain of the road in the dark I made for what looked like, or rather smelt like, dead horses or bullocks—fine landmarks, an excellent guide on the veldt when one is in difficulty.

June 16th.—At headquarters. Sir H. Rawlinson is spending much time in helping me, Lord Roberts lending himself with his usual grace and kindliness, such as passing through one door instead of another so as to suit the requirements of light and shade. This living portrait which I made of Lord Roberts, I suggested to him we would gladly send to Lady Roberts with his permission. To this he consented with pleasure, he said. Then as I wished to photograph him on his beautiful charger, he again smilingly consented, besides leaving off his helmet and wearing his forage cap when asked to do so. The soldiers adore him. There is never the slightest murmur against him ; he is ever courteous, kind and considerate, and withal firm as a rock.

June 17th.—We have sold our horses and Cape cart, saddles, tent and general camping outfit, and are now waiting the end of the campaign. Some think that Botha will surrender and that De Wet is surrounded. Many rumours afloat. Botha pushed a few miles further from Pretoria when we again fought him. We commandeered some Basuto ponies to-day and rode out to Wunderbaum and the caves, twenty miles in return. Stopped at a Boer house for lunch—much entertained by the hostess and her children. Here at last we get some fresh butter. I bought all they had, some five pounds, and put it into my saddlebags. Before leaving this charming district we stopped to photograph the house, and pretty ten-year old daughter playing with her pet lambs, dog, and cat, which followed her about in the most amusing manner. Then I proceeded to the caves, taking with me twine and candles. On the way were to be seen many holes dug by gold prospectors. Passing a Kaffir kraal of several huts, we had quite a diverting time snapshotting the half-naked inmates. They were adorned with beads and brass ornaments, of some of which I relieved the ladies by paying a fair price. As for the little tots, pickaninies, they were an endless source of delightful amusement to me. These people are perfectly happy when with her Majesty's subjects, but are ill-treated by the Boers. A helmet is always greeted with a grin. After bidding them goodbye, they raised their arms and continued loudly crying, "Inkoos! Baba! Sakubona!" It means, "Chief! Father! I see you!" One man followed

DUKE OF WESTMINSTER AND GENERAL FRENCH AT PRETORIA.

18

THREE THOUSAND BRITISH SOLDIERS RELEASED FROM PRISON AT PRETORIA
BEING RE-ARMED IN THE PUBLIC SQUARE.

to guide us to the caves. About a mile further on, not far from a kopje, a good clump of trees indicated the locality. After dismounting and giving our horses in charge of the attendant, we lit our candles and let out our ball of twine to guide us back through the complex windings. All quite interesting, these caves, but ordinary and not half so large or interesting as those I discovered in America, at the Natural Bridge in Virginia. Nearly all the way down we amused ourselves chipping off the roof and sides bits of gold-bearing quartz. It was easy to follow the reef. No doubt some day soon these caves will be worked, especially as Dame Nature has already tumbled around the gold ore to invite trade. After scrambling about, pushing through most uncomfortably small holes (being rewarded once in a while, however, by coming out into larger rooms), we gave it up, especially as we found that our time had run out and one of our party had strayed far ahead. After much shouting we finally got together again and left these fascinating underground haunts to the bats, that were now wide awake and persistent in coming up against us. Two of these we caught, and my assistant placed them inside his helmet. As nature had deprived him of his hair, it is a mystery to me still how he stood the fuss and scratchings on his bare pate. Every now and then, while stopping for breath, we would hear the flap of their wings against the helmet. It was awfully funny, especially his frantic endeavours to regain his pets when his headgear came off while he was trying to save himself from a fall. Daylight again. Quickly saddling our Basuto ponies, we strike across country, keeping a sharp look-out for any unpleasant *rencontre*. Night

came on rather too suddenly as we delayed at a Boer
farm talking with them, trying to draw them out.
We had eleven miles yet to go before reaching
Pretoria, now quite dark and no moon, and the road
hard to see. Twice the pony came to knee in holes.
My two companions were not quite so lucky. My
assistant behind soon followed suit, crashing to the
ground, the little Basuto rolling over him by way of
amusement or spite. Later, No. 3 performed a
remarkable acrobatic feat as his beast did his turn.
Our friend unfortunately injured his knee, which
soon swelled to the size of the calf of his leg, poor
chap. It would have been very much worse, of
course, had he been dragged, but the little beast
stopped short on regaining its feet and stood gazing
complacently at his fallen lord, who now had to vary
his style by riding *à la* Dame. No further accidents,
and after occasionally being called to halt by our
mounted patrols and giving a fair account of ourselves which allowed us to proceed, we got to our
stables just three minutes before the time was up
by when all men were required to be in unless upon
patrol work.

June 18*th.*—Baden-Powell is here at last. He
quietly reported at headquarters to Lord Roberts,
who, hearing of his being in the vicinity, ordered
out his guard of yeomanry to escort him in. Lord
Roberts and his guards missing them, they met at
the gates, and, thanks again to our Chief and Lord
Settrington, the Biograph is able to show Lord
Roberts shaking hands with General Baden-Powell
at the gate, marching up to the house, followed by
the Staff on foot.

Now we feel like going home, but still delay,

BOERS ENCRUSTING THE PUBLIC BUILDINGS GIVING UP THEIR ARMS.

LORD ROBERTS COMING FROM CHURCH | THE FIRST SUNDAY
IN PRETORIA.

hoping that the war may end and that the final
ceremony may take place, namely, the annexation of
the Transvaal. It is now past midnight, and while
sitting at my table scribbling, my feet have frozen
hard. I must take a run in the open and risk a
sentry or two to get my blood up.

God bless our Queen and firmly establish her
beneficent rule.

Johannisburg, June 27, 1900.—Since my last
letter we have been riding here and there in search
of excitement, and many things have befallen us. I
saw Lord Roberts and thanked him for all his kindness to me, and was advised by him not to wait any
longer for the annexation ceremony, that event
being indefinitely postponed by reason of De Wet and
Botha having captured a convoy, greatly to their
renewed encouragement. We clasped hands, and
after Lord Roberts and Staff had written their names
upon my flag of truce, I took my departure, shaking
the dust of Pretoria off my shoes in my thankfulness
to get away.

On by rail to Johannisburg, expecting to be nipped
by the Boers. The train in front of us was fired on
for several hours, and we were told we went at our
own risk, but I feared that if we didn't push on, the
bridge would be again blown up and another long
delay ensue. My man, who had only returned a
day or two before from a trip to Bloemfontein with
our films, had the unenviable experience of seeing
the bridge over which he had just crossed blown up.
The engineer never even waited to see the Boers,
but put on full speed, much to the relief of the men
on board. We felt that we must keep a good look-
out as we passed over the same ground; but nothing

of note happened, except that we got stuck for three
and a half hours on the open veldt. Our engine
having broken down, we had to wait its return from
Elansfontein, where it had gone for repairs or
exchange. Meanwhile we scanned the darkening
horizon with our field-glasses for Boers, and found
them, four in number, on horseback, watching us.
I cannot say I felt altogether comfortable. We were
but a mere handful of men, and hardly able to defend
the train. Our officer friends had a quiet consultation, and the senior officer took charge and got the
few men together and ready. Night came on, and
bitterly cold it grew, none daring to sleep. Several
of our men on guard lay down and watched the sky-
line for Boers. At about nine we heard the distant
whistle of the locomotive, and knew our release had
come. Soon we were away, and reached Johannisburg at about 10.30, when we were glad to retire
and rest our weary bones.

Next day, June 28th.—We thoroughly canvassed
the city through the open-hearted hospitable mining
manager of the Meyer and Charlton, Mr. Kurt
Baswitz, who spent several days showing me the
ins and outs of this marvellous and world-renowned
gold reef, and the processes used to extract the
precious metal. I was deeply interested, and grateful to him and his associates for their trouble and
kindness. The Ferari ·Mines have also much to
boast of in excellent machinery, all in good working
order, under the able management of Mr. Walker,
who, by the way, got his compound Kaffir manager
to turn out three hundred half-naked savages to
dance a war dance for me. There was so much dust
raised in their wild gyrations that it had to be

LORD ROBERTS' BODYGUARD.

PRESIDENT KRUGER'S HOUSE, PRETORIA.

repeated on less dusty ground. It was a fine sight, but it proved rather difficult to secure the best portion of this unique dance. Rider Haggard's description of a war dance cannot be surpassed, so I must refer my friends to any of his South African books on the subject. Several Kaffirs are placed in front of the warriors and hammer at huge, crudely made xylophones, ranging from a deep bass to a high treble—wonderfully musical and pleasing to the ear. There's one thing you may always be sure of when it is a question of Kaffir singing, that you will never hear a discordant sound. It is wild, weird, grand.

They discuss the enemy in a monotonous chant, pointing occasionally to the distant hills where they propose to attack and eat them up, and gradually work themselves into a frenzy, singing furiously, and dashing their assegai and shields to the ground, leaping into the air and stamping on their imaginary enemies. It makes the cold chills creep down your back—so awfully realistic does it appear. They seem in deadly earnest, and keep on and on while the musicians hammer away with the deep undertone of the tom-tom, keeping this up until nearly faint from exhaustion.

Our time is well spent aboveground among the mining machinery, and to vary the programme we take a run down a mine in a sort of elongated bucket, which is used to hoist out the water, among other things. Four of us, packed like herrings in a barrel, would go down with a rush at a signal from our cicerones, Mr. Conly or Mr. Baswitz, and soon lose sight of the opening as the angle of the reef changed. We reached a level, 1,700 feet deep, and wandered

about in surprisingly dry tunnels, soon becoming
absorbed in the account given us of the manner in
which the ore is mined, which seems to be a curious
hard conglomerate containing quartzose pebbles,
around which the gold is found invisible to the naked
eye. After making a few sketches we reascend,
and gladly welcome the sunlight after our long
underground walk.

Through the courteous hospitality of our friends,
we enjoyed a sumptuous repast that evening—an
" at home "—which was a decided improvement on
our veldt fare. Next day we were driven about in
Mr. Baswitz' splendid carriage and pair, and shown
the most wonderful city in the world for its years—
a perfect Eldorado. These grand palatial edifices are
furnished regardless of cost, and money seems to be
a very ordinary thing here. You become satiated
with gold dust, gold amalgam, and gold bars ; in the
very streets and squares gold reef outcroppings may
be seen, and many a householder has gold in his
cellar.

The people are large-hearted, and it is a relief to
find penuriousness an unknown trait in the character
of the inhabitant of Johannisburg. He is ready to
spend money like water for a good thing, or even
to help a penniless brainy chap who may have come
out to seek his fortune.

The city seems to greatly grieve over the loss of
its able mining engineer, Major Seymour, who was
shot in the defence of his country. He had formed
a volunteer corps, and before Lord Roberts arrived at
Johannisburg was shot in or near that city at some
engagement.

My last evening in Johannisburg was spent in a

AT 8.30 THE CAVALCADE MOVED ON.

FRONT FIRING LINE, BRITISH INFANTRY.

unique and delightful way. My friend, Lieutenant Bates, invited me to meet Colonel Curtis and several of his officer friends and dine inside the city fort, giving me the seat of honour beside the Colonel, which I greatly enjoyed. We were about thirty or forty at a long table, lit from above by electric lights. The fact that the room, or vault, was bomb-proof within the walls of the fort made the event all the more odd. After a good military dinner and excellent wine, we all adjourned to the commandeered home of Lieutenant Bates (who, by the way, is Crown Prosecutor for Johannisburg). There we had a royal night of it. It is wonderful how much talent can be dug out from our British officers at such times. But the best of friends must part, and on the morrow we packed up again. I wrote to Lord Roberts' headquarters to ask if anything was going to happen.

On July 3rd came the kind reply to my letter :

" No hurry, probably month at least.—Colonel Sir H. RAWLINSON."

So off we went a few days later, and got on towards De Aar to change for Kimberley, thence to Capetown.

The trip took nearly a week, but was interesting in part, especially Kimberley. We left on Monday, travelling day and night, and only reached Capetown on Saturday—Whew !

But to return to De Aar Junction, where we had to get off the main line. We were obliged to get into the guard's van, which we found devoid of springs and very dusty. We luckily got some hot water from the engine as night came on and made our tea, and wound up by sleeping (or trying to) on the shelf. We first tried to both sleep, head to foot, but as it grew unbearably narrow, my companion took to the dusty floor. The goods train stopped everywhere during the night, and not being able to even shut our eyes, we amused ourselves by watching the splendid moon as we tramped up and down on the veldt, keeping close to the rails for fear of a sudden start. We could easily hear when the other train was coming for which we were waiting on a siding, as this system is nearly all on the narrow gauge and single line.

Next morning we got in at 4.30, and were hustled out by moonlight into a vacant waiting-room. We soon procured some hot water, and refreshed ourselves with some ground coffee made, like tea, in our cups.

At seven we commenced to tramp the city, then only just getting light, and soon found our way towards the Diamond huge quarry open cuts, perfectly volcanic in its appearance; in fact, the theory many people hold here is, that these diamond pits are a series of long extinct volcanic craters which have been instrumental in forming these diamonds through heat and pressure, as the grey clay containing the pebbles goes down, and is found at great depths in shafts, and nowhere else.

At nine I had presented my letter from the Hon. Cecil Rhodes, in which he requests that I be shown over and "given every assistance," and soon we were flying from one part of the country to another, visiting the splendid offices containing the cut diamonds to the value of hundreds of thousands of pounds. From there we went a distance of two miles to the pulsators, where the diamonds are mechanically

J. S. Smidt.   J. F. Debeer.   Dr. W. C. Sholtz.

AN OLD-FASHIONED STAGE-COACH WAS BROUGHT INTO REQUISITION.

MY CAPE CART, REQUISITIONED BY LORD ROBERTS FOR PEACE NEGOTIATIONS
WITH LOUIS BOTHA, DRIVEN BY THE MILITARY SECRETARY, CAPTAIN
WATERFIELD, TO THE BOER LINES.

picked out.   For years they had to employ hundreds
of people to sort out diamonds, and now, by the
simplest discovery made by a nameless *employé*,
the whole diamond business takes on a new phase,
and becomes the most fabulously important money-
making scheme in the world.   A pot of grease
did it.

Mr. Lambert, foreman of the works, who was
unfortunately killed by a shell exploding in his

LORD ROBERTS' AUTOGRAPH.

room at the Grand Hotel in Kimberley, had been
experimenting on pulsators, or inclined tables over
which water and pebbles, graduated through meshes,
were made to fall or slide as the tables shivered and
shook laterally.   A young *employé*, whose hands
were very greasy, had run his hand across the plate,
and then, lo and behold! a diamond had stopped.
Quickly dabbing on a lot of grease, he found that all
the diamonds, large and small, were arrested in their

rush. Strange to say, scarcely a diamond can escape being caught by the grease, while everything else is carried on and past these sparkling gems. The large ones are picked off and the grease treated with hot caustic soda, forming a watery soap, and thus saving the little gems.

We next visited the huge fields where the ore is brought up from the shafts. Here, by the way, Cecil Rhodes stowed away and fed many thousand women and children while the city was being daily bombarded.

The clay, soft and hard, is thrown out and spread for the sun and weather to gradually disintegrate. A careful and sharp eye could make a little fortune in discovering diamonds, for after eighteen months the clay crumbles to dust, and in breaking up it may not be impossible to find a few big stones.

All this is carried to the washing department, of which there are several, at a mile or so apart, where the ore is washed free of the very fines, and all gravelly stuff sifted through rotary sieves, the larger going on to the " Gates " crushers, whence they return to be washed. The circular washers then receive the stuff, and so on, the pebbles having been all extracted from the two kinds of clay. They are then sent down to the pulsators, and, as already explained, the diamonds are extracted.

While driving around we saw huge iron towers, from which searchlights are in constant use, sweeping the diamond fields to see if there is any one searching among the lumps of clay for the gems. These searchlights were invaluable during the Kimberley siege, to watch the approach of the enemy and give

BADEN-POWELL IS HERE AT LAST.   LORD ROBERTS WITH BADEN-POWELL
ENTERING HEADQUARTERS.

20

our people warning. On one of these towers Colonel
Kekewitch, who had command of the military forces
in that city, had an observation tower built even
above the searchlight, and one and all of these
towers were connected with this one (as headquarters) telephonically.

THE FLAG OF TRUCE.

The people here worship Rhodes, and had it not
been for him they say the city could not have
held out. He did everything. His money went
like water. He fed thousands gratis. The De
Beer Company loaned and gave out huge loads of
boiler plates for defences, and finally built " Long

Cecil" at their works with what material they had. This gun was successful, among the first few shots fired, in hitting the nose of the Boers' big, destructive, far-ranging "Long Tom." One picture loaned me for reproduction by one of the unfortunates within the city, shows the women and children waiting their turn to go down the mine, in mortal terror of this Long Tom and other possible shells. Another shows their release after several weeks' imprisonment underground, at a depth of 1,400 feet. Many are now suffering terribly from rheumatism, which the doctors fear is permanent in many cases.

A snap-shot shows Long Cecil guarded in the city barracks. Its Boer rival, Long Tom, had to undergo amputation, which operation was performed in Pretoria, the gun having become so battered that over two feet had to be cut off before it could be used again. This repairing took some time, and gave the inhabitants a temporary surcease of hostilities from that particular source.

There is lots to tell about Kimberley, but time won't allow, so on our way to the railway station we amused ourselves counting the huge placards announcing the fact that the American Biograph would be exhibited nightly to show the war pictures.

Passing the bridge we noticed a small British flag —or handkerchief flag—very much the worse for weather and wear ; and finding the owner, I got my companion to climb the telegraph pole, while I took the easiest (?) job in quieting the proprietor's qualms. The flag looked so dejected and forlorn that I thought it my duty to take it away, and in the act destroy the impression already made on the passers by, that our flag, however small and insignificant, could appear anything else but triumphant; so I bagged the game.   This flag, among several others not now there, was part of the celebration of the relief of Kimberley.

From Kimberley we made a straight shoot to

"LONG CECIL"—BUILT IN KIMBERLEY DURING THE SIEGE.

Capetown, only stopping long enough at De Aar to see how many more graves there were, and taking some snap-shots of the poor chaps' last resting-place.

Capetown, July 13th.—We cabled to our respective families and my London partner. Saturday, Sunday, Monday, Tuesday passed, and no answer came until

Wednesday morning, just in time to get their welcome messages before we sail on the *Carisbrooke Castle*, July 18, 1900.

As a fitting wind-up to our South African campaign we visit the great Post Office at Capetown, under military rule, and are lost in wonder as to how the army, with its thousand branches, ever receive their letters, especially as our men are constantly being changed about from one brigade to another.

I am indebted to Major G. W. Treble, who has full charge of all this work for Africa, for the most interesting account of how it is done. He said :—

" To begin with, there is every week an average of 750,000 letters, besides tons of parcels, and everybody growls about not getting their letters in time. They may be thankful to get them at all, what with men changing their regiment, De Wet's little fun in destroying three weeks' batch of 2,000 bags, and a single line only for thousands of miles around the country.

" A gentleman called at the Capetown offices and begged to be allowed to go through the mail which had just come in, as he would know his letters in a minute and save us much trouble. I was willing of course if he chose to spend the time, and escorting him to the great halls I pointed to a huge pyramid of sacks, and told him he would have to work through that first, then go into the next room and there he would find a similar lot. He, of course, declined to undertake the work and gracefully retired. Yes, it is wonderful how we ever got out of this apparently chaotic state of things. It all comes out straight, though, with system and hard work.

"It is funny to see clever portrait sketches and photographs on the envelopes, placed there to assist us in identifying the lost ones who have shifted over to some other regiment and forgotten to write home about the change."

MILITARY POSTMASTER, CAPETOWN (MAJOR TREBLE).

It is wonderful how greatly the penny postage has helped to fill up the mail bags. All the Tommies and their sweethearts know of the reduction, unfortunately for the officials, and no place is more popular than the field post office. That much sought after place is haunted day and night. You lose a friend—why! you just send to the post office, not the pub. At Ladysmith I ascertained that over twenty tons of letters were in the town in less than three days after the relief—*i.e.*, twelve ox-waggons and two mule-waggons heavily loaded.

It is with the deepest feeling of gratitude that I now watch the receding shores of South Africa, and know that I am on my way home after a ten months' fever-heat of excitement, toil and peril.

These war experiences have been of a most complex nature, but I am conscious of one supreme impression deepening as my mind reviews the whole bewildering throng. It is my admiration of the British soldiery and commanders together with a prophetic sense of their ability to maintain the high standard of an advanced civilisation, which they have so signally evinced, as well in peace as in war.

UNWIN BROTHERS, THE GRESHAM PRESS, WOKING AND LONDON.

WHAT IS NORMAN and STACEY'S PLAN of Furnishing?

It is a clever scheme (endorsed even by Mr. Labouchere, of *Truth*), now known and adopted in all parts of the English-speaking world, which enables you to Furnish your House or Flat throughout, from Drawing-room to Kitchen (even to the extent of Linens, Silver, Cutlery, Blinds, &c.), out of income, without disturbing your capital by (instead of paying Cash) dividing the whole amount into 6, 12, 24, or 36 equal monthly payments.

During the above-mentioned period you can, of course, at any time (should you wish it) pay off the amount and avail yourself of the cash discount.

NORMAN and STACEY ARE FREQUENTLY ASKED why they do not publish a fixed scale of payments. Their reply thereto is that, in view of the fact that their customers principally belong to the higher classes, experience has taught them that customers much prefer to submit their own terms of payment.

There is scarcely a recognised paper of any standing that has not during the last few years considered it its duty to call attention to "NORMAN and STACEY'S Instalment Plan of Furnishing."

Ladies should make a point of paying a visit to Norman and Stacey's Show Rooms, to compare quality and prices with other large houses.

THE DAILY TELEGRAPH says:—

"The Jury has awarded its Diploma of honour to Messrs. Norman and Stacey (Ltd.) for their Exhibit of Furniture. This is the highest award in its particular class."

NORMAN and STACEY (Ltd.),
118, QUEEN VICTORIA STREET, E.C.

All goods marked in plain figures.

Country orders receive special attention. Free delivery.

Inspection solicited.

A beautiful catalogue in colours is given upon personal application.

N.B.—In 1894 we originated the Free Life Insurance System of Furnishing. Beware of imitators.

Mr. W. Kennedy-Laurie Dickson writes : "I am more than delighted with the Ever-Ready Flash Light. It is splendid."